the view from my kitchen window

The View From My Kitchen Window

A Memoir with Recipes

Julie Kalt Gale

illustrations by
Tobias Gale

additional illustrations by
Julie Kalt Gale

LIBRARY OF
CONGRESS
SURPLUS
DUPLICATE

Epigraph Books
Rhinebeck, New York

Paperback ISBN 978-1-960090-17-1

Library of Congress Control Number 2023911562

Illustrations by Tobias Gale
Additional illustrations by Julie Kalt Gale
Book and cover design by Colin Rolfe

Epigraph Books
22 East Market Street, Suite 304
Rhinebeck, NY 12572
(845) 876-4861
epigraphps.com

This book is dedicated to my dear husband, Peter,
and the beautiful family we have created:
Adam (and Lacey),
Zachary (and Roza),
Tobias (and Brittany),
Elizabeth,
and our newest additions,
Artemus and Kazimir, sons of Zach and Roza.

CONTENTS

PREFACE

I come from a long line of storytellers. The dinner table has always been the stage for the stories of my life. My grandparents, parents, brother, and I have all delighted in telling and retelling the stories of our family. As we sit around the Thanksgiving or Passover table, the younger generation does not much enjoy hearing, one more time, the story of how so-and-so did such-and-such. Yet—here it comes again—to my great delight.

This book of memories was born at a time when my parents were old enough that I could see the end coming, and it was a way to preserve this piece of them for their grandchildren. Stories were not the only delicious thing served at those tables; the food rivaled the stories and made them a bit more bearable. I also come from a long line of great cooks. I truly believe it is a gene that runs through our family and has not stopped with me.

My four children are wonderful cooks, as well as amazing human beings (*said she, modestly*). My dear husband, Peter, was not brought up in a family who loved to cook and this is what has made him, all the more, the wonderful audience that he is. He enjoys the stories and the food that accompanies them so much and never tires of my efforts in both story and food.

It is my hope that by writing this book, these memories of my family of unique characters and the recipes for the food we loved to cook and eat will become a treasured addition to your family's heirloom recipes as well!

INTRODUCTION

I believe that I am most comfortable in my skin when I am cooking. My earliest memories are in the kitchen or at the kitchen table. I began making my breakfast for myself starting at age five. I could barely reach the counter, but I would get my cereal, bowl, spoon, and milk—and sit down and eat. When I think back on this, I cannot imagine allowing such a small child to be alone in the morning before school. At the time, I was pretty proud of myself and didn't know that other children had it any other way. My dad was usually away all night, delivering babies, and my mother was a late sleeper. I was responsible for getting myself dressed, fed, and out the door to the school bus—pretty impressive, I must say. When I was six, we moved to a big house in a wealthy neighborhood with a live-in housekeeper. That was the end of my solo mornings and the beginning of what might be called my "privileged" upbringing.

When my daughter Elizabeth, now known as Eli, was seventeen, she wrote a song with the line, "Well, maybe I'm privileged, maybe I'm crazy…." Yes, she was privileged but definitely not crazy. We raised her along with our three sons in suburban Westchester County, New York and spent our summers in the Hudson Valley. By the time Elizabeth, who is the youngest by eight years, was finishing elementary school, we began to understand that we all needed to leave the entitled world of Larchmont and live a simpler more rewarding life at our weekend home in rural Hillsdale, New York. Elizabeth spent the next eight years in a magical Waldorf school less than ten minutes from home. Hawthorne Valley Waldorf School is integrated into the life of Hawthorne Valley Farm—with cows, chickens, pigs, and farmland. She did not live the privileged life that her brothers grew up in, but she understood that she had much more than most children her age. I believe that her understanding of her privileges is what separated her from most teenagers in her social stratosphere.

I admit that I in no way had this sensitivity when I was her age. I grew up in suburban Long Island in a fancy house in a fancy neighborhood with fancy furniture and fancy parents. However, living in a big, empty house in Woodbury did not make me feel privileged. My parents always hired live-in help which I understood at the time was indeed a privilege of sorts. These ladies were nice enough, but none were English-speaking, so although there was always someone home when I got off the school bus, they were completely unable to ask me how my day was or what I learned at school. These South American women came through the house as though by a revolving door, rarely staying for more than six months and therefore never learning enough English to have a conversation. I did, however, learn to speak kitchen-Spanish, which as it turned out served me well my whole life.

My daily routine while growing up was that I would come home, throw my things on the front bench, and cook myself a snack. I would cook up some Rice-A-Roni, an omelet—or my very favorite, Rice Krispies treats, which I ate warm right out of the pot. I sat at the kitchen table and ate my snack by myself as I read a magazine. I truly relished the time I spent in the kitchen cooking for myself. As I think about it now, I don't believe that I have ever had to cook for myself ever again. When I left college, I lived at home until I was married and have been cooking for my husband and my children ever since. I realize now that when I was a child, I had to cook to feed myself—but cooking literally fed my soul as well as my belly.

This book traces the path of that child, who in a sense cooked to live—and the path of the woman she became, who lived to cook. These are the stories of my life and the recipes that fed my soul.

CHAPTER 1

244 TWIN LANE EAST,
WANTAGH, NEW YORK
1956-1962

When I was an infant, my parents bought a small postwar home in the Levitt-built community of Wantagh, Long Island. I remember it as sweet and compact, with conveniences such as a carport adjacent to the snug kitchen. The kitchen window over the sink looked out into the carport. This gave my mother the view she needed when I was having a snack out there.

Just inside the house from the carport was a small playroom. The little fenced-in backyard had a tree swing and easy access for my best friend, Kenny Milne, who lived next door. Kenny and I spent our days running in and out of our houses, playing in the sandbox with my pet turtle, Susan, and very naughtily picking the neighbor's tulips. One memorable incident involved our disobeying

Mom and Me, 1956

strict orders and crossing the street to the neighborhood playground. We were both given a spanking for that escapade—my first and last, but probably not his.

Kenny's mother could always be counted on for after-school snacks, such as Cheese Doodles, Devil Dogs, and our beloved cherry Kool-Aid. I was not allowed such unwholesome treats at home, so naturally, I requested them every time we played at his house. However, we were only allowed to have the Kool-Aid outside at our little table under their carport. Those cherry-red stains were forever!

When I was about five years old, on an early spring morning I looked out my bedroom window and saw Kenny dressed in a yellow bunny-suit delivering an Easter basket to my door. Easter was a foreign and forbidden holiday in our Jewish household, and that was the first and only time I have ever had an Easter-bunny delivery. I remember how delighted I was to tear open the yellow and pink cellophane wrapper that enveloped the foil-wrapped chocolate eggs and marshmallow bunny.

Kenny was the perfect next-door neighbor, always available yet close enough to go home when we were not having fun anymore. There is something very special about having a best friend right next door!

The homes on the block were all cookie-cutter designs that the renowned builder, Bill Levitt, had designed for ease, comfort—and most of all, affordability. My parents bought the house in 1957 for $11,700! I was recently in the area and returned to see the house and the neighborhood. Fifty years later it was still a charming street with neat homes, well-cared-for gardens, and a central playground.

However, much to my disappointment, my old home was the only neglected one on the block. There were empty tuna cans (presumably for cats), bowling balls, and turned-over garden sculptures in the yard—the very worst of which was a statue of a dog peeing on a fire hydrant. I held my breath, found my courage, and rang the door- bell. A scruffy young man who wreaked of pot answered the door. It turned out that he was the grandson of the owner who bought the house from my

Mom, Dad, and Me 1956

father. I didn't ask to go inside, and he didn't invite me to do so. I told him that I had lived there until I was six years old, which did not seem to interest him in the slightest, so I hurried back to the car.

It was sad to see my earliest memories literally gone up in a puff of smoke, but the rest of Twin Lane East was just as lovely as I had remembered it. That helped to reduce some of the disappointment in seeing my lovely little house in such disarray.

My earliest food memories are associated with that little house. It was there that I was introduced to the joys of eating lobster—which I apparently pronounced "lopis" and, alternately, "lockster"—and the horror of eating baked beans. My father would place a single baked bean on the side of my plate, close his eyes, and "magically," the bean would disappear before he opened his eyes. I was thoroughly nauseated eating even one little baked bean, but I did it just to win his approval and his supposed disbelief that the baked bean had vanished.

I must admit, I still get a little queasy when I open a can of baked beans. However, I discovered that in order for me to actually enjoy the taste of baked beans, I must make my own, and that entirely changes my attitude towards them. I can even eat them without saying, *ta-da!*

HOMEMADE BAKED BEANS

INGREDIENTS

2 cups dried navy beans
6 cups water
4 slices thick-cut bacon,
   chopped
1 onion, sliced in half
1 Tbs. Worcestershire sauce
1 tsp. liquid smoke
1 cup dark molasses
1/2 cup maple syrup
1/4 cup dark brown sugar,
   packed
2 Tbs. Dijon mustard
1 Tbs. sea salt
1 tsp. black pepper

DIRECTIONS

Boil the beans in the water for 10 minutes and then allow to soak overnight or, preferably, place the beans and water in a large pressure cooker and cook for 20 minutes. Heat the oven to 300°. Place the cooked beans and then the rest of the ingredients into a large bowl and mix thoroughly. Pour into a bean pot or a covered ceramic casserole dish, adding enough water to cover the mixture by about an inch. Cover and cook for 5 hours, stirring every half hour and add water if it begins to dry out. Uncover for the last hour. Taste for seasoning.

SERVES 8

Dad and Me

In contrast to the difficult time I had eating baked beans, I have very fond memories of eating lobster. I recall, at age four, sitting at our little table off the kitchen in the room that I believe was called the den, where my father taught me how to twist the body to remove the tail and then twist the claws to pull out all the meat.

I suppose that I have always enjoyed working for my food, which is certainly required for lobster, crab, and shrimp—my three favorite foods of the sea. My horoscope sign is Cancer the Crab, perhaps one of the reasons why I have always adored eating crustaceans. I have noticed for many years that whenever I eat lobster or crab, I am poked to the point of bleeding from the creature. I suspect that this is the price we pay for eating them.

I believe that one of the first times I ate lobster was on Cape Cod during frightening Hurricane Donna in 1960. We had rented a small house on the beach, and the storm became so intense that my mother and our babysitter were terrified. I remember my father, the doctor, giving them each an injection of valium or something like it. The size of the needle scared me more than the sounds of the hurricane!

I remember my father cooking dinner that night because the two women were comatose. We had perfectly cooked fresh lobster with lemon butter—my favorite! We never went to Cape Cod again.

Mom and Me

Speaking of seafood, my parents had some very good friends during this time of my life, and their best friends were Aunt Harriet and Uncle Gene. They lived in Woodmere, which was at the epicenter of the Long Island Jewish community.

However, in the same way as my parents, they were not at all interested in being part of organized religion and did not follow any of the kosher dietary laws. My parents went so far in the opposite direction that shellfish and pork were the primary foods on their table (mine too, I must admit!).

Aunt Harriet taught my mother one of our favorite party foods that we served to guests when we lived in Wantagh. It was a simple spread with frozen crab (fresh crab was not easily available), prepared chili sauce, Hellmann's mayonnaise—and oh so sophisticated—Madras curry powder. I loved it and still do!

AUNT HARRIET'S CURRIED CRAB

INGREDIENTS

1 lb. crab meat, picked over
2 celery stalks, finely chopped
2 hard-boiled eggs, chopped
2 Tbs. bottled Chili Sauce
2-3 Tbs. Hellman's mayonnaise
1-2 tsp. Madras curry powder
1 tsp. fresh lemon or lime juice
1 tsp. fresh chives, minced

DIRECTIONS

Place the crab, celery and eggs in a medium bowl and mix gently. In a small bowl combine the rest of the ingredients (except the chives) and then incorporate the sauce in to the crab mixture being careful to leave the crab pieces as large as possible. Sprinkle with the chives and refrigerate until ready to serve. Serve on water crackers.

SERVES 4-6

The most memorable treat from my early childhood was my first taste of tempura-fried zucchini. I was playing in the backyard, trying to climb to the top of what seemed like a very high, white picket fence. My parents were expecting guests for dinner and brought out a plate of fried zucchini for me to sample.

Now, as a mother myself, I think perhaps it was an easy way to get me down off the fence without a fight. I was very reluctant to try the zucchini at first but was soon persuaded when I saw my parents diving in and crunching them enthusiastically. My mother had cut the zucchinis into long spears and dipped them in a tempura batter before frying them. The first bite had me hooked!

They were so scrumptious; the crunch of the batter, the soft flesh of the sweet zucchini, and the salty sharp tang of the soy sauce dip combined to make an irresistible treat. I couldn't get enough of them, and I must admit, I still have trouble resisting fried food of any type.

Mom and me, 1959

ZUCCHINI IN TEMPURA BATTER

INGREDIENTS

6 small zucchinis, sliced in long,
  1/2-inch-thick spears
1 egg yolk
2 cups ice water
Pinch of baking soda
1 2/3 cup all-purpose flour
Extra flour for dipping
Vegetable oil for frying
1/4 cup mirin (sweet sake)
1/4 cup tamari sauce
1/4 cup rice wine vinegar

DIRECTIONS

Heat enough vegetable oil in a wok to come 1/3 of the way up the side of a wok. Heat the oil over moderately high heat until it reaches 375° on a frying thermometer. Meanwhile, mix together the egg yolk, ice water, baking soda, and all-purpose flour to form a thin batter. Dredge the zucchinis in the extra flour to form a thin coating and then dip them, 4 or 5 pieces at a time, into the batter and then into the hot oil. Combine the mirin, tamari, and rice vinegar in a small bowl for the dipping sauce. Turn the zucchinis in the oil so that they brown on all sides, and drain them on a wire rack. Serve immediately with dipping sauce.

SERVES 4

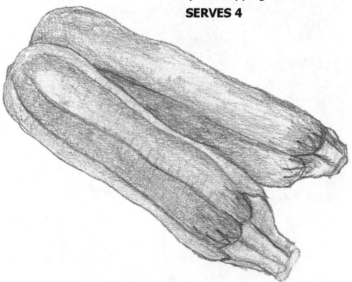

Mom and Dad

Even as a young couple of very modest means, my parents enjoyed entertaining. When I was a young child, they often had people over to dinner. It was much too expensive to go out to eat and much more fun to have guests at home. They continued to entertain at home until close to the very end.

My parents were both enthusiastic cooks and had very international tastes, which was fueled by their beloved *Time/Life Foods of the World* series of cookbooks. This series continues to be my go-to whenever I am looking for a recipe. However, one of their best-loved hors d'oeuvres, which was originally Craig Claiborne's, was the very American: Parmesan-Onion Rounds. My mother met Craig Claiborne at a food shop in Greenwich Village, and she was so thrilled that she began making these yummy goodies all the time. (I think that she did so partly as a conversation starter so she could mention her connection to him.)

These hors d'oeuvres are very inexpensive to make but very labor-intensive and time-consuming. And consume is what you will do! I can easily eat five or six at a time. At a Christmas party I was catering, one guest came into the kitchen to meet me after tasting these and declared them "divine"! I have to agree, they are *heavenly*.

PARMESAN-ONION ROUNDS

INGREDIENTS

Best-quality, very thinly-sliced white bread (such as Arnold's)

Onions, sliced as thinly as possible (carefully use a Japanese mandolin slicer)

Hellmann's Mayonnaise

Freshly-grated Parmesan cheese

Fresh parsley, finely chopped

Sweet paprika

DIRECTIONS

Preheat the broiler. Using a 2-inch metal biscuit cutter, cut as many circles from the bread as possible. You will want to prepare enough for 4 servings per person, which is why there are no amounts given for each ingredient. Spread the circles generously and evenly with the mayonnaise. Cover the mayonnaise with a slice of the onion, leaving the edges to brown. Sprinkle with the cheese and then with the parsley and paprika. Place the rounds next to each other on cookie sheets. Broil, watching closely, until the cheese and bread become lightly browned. Serve hot.

My parents were both very good cooks, but each had their own style of prep and clean-up (e.g., they never cleaned up!). My mother was a very precise cook who relied entirely on recipes and required every ingredient in a recipe before attempting it. For instance, she and I were all ready to make cookies together that contained walnuts, but she did not have walnuts, only pecans. When I outlandishly suggested she substitute pecans for the walnuts, she threw up her hands and left the kitchen.

My mother inherited a lot of her mother's idiosyncrasies, which are called *mishagas* in Yiddish, in the kitchen. Nana, as we called my mother's mother, was a total neat-freak and had the incredibly tidy habit of cleaning as she cooked, so that when dinner was ready there was nothing in the kitchen that required cleaning. She literally had no garbage pails in her apartment, so whenever something needed to be thrown out, such as a used tissue, one had to go to the incinerator down the hall to get rid of it! You can't make these things up!

Everything Nana made tasted delicious—simple, wholesome but really delicious. Nana was born in Prussia and came to America when she was twelve years old. She was sent to an immigrant training program on New York City's Lower East Side called The Educational Alliance. It was there that she was taught that in order to be a good American, she would need to give up her immigrant traditions and do everything American-style. That included how she cooked, so everything she cooked used good American ingredients.

Nana, Papa, and Dad, 1959

I especially loved her ridiculously simple elbow macaroni. It has to be *Mrs. Mueller's brand* mixed with canned tomato sauce (which must be *Del Monte's*) and topped with American cheese (which must be *Kraft American Cheese*). It was baked until the cheese had just begun to brown, and it is one of the true comfort foods of my childhood. She invented it as a way to add a little protein to one of the few foods that her fussy children would eat. I am sure that she would have been surprised at how little protein the cheese really had. Those were the days before manufacturers needed to disclose everything. I remember visiting her in my college days, and I am ashamed to admit that I probably had four helpings of it!

NANA'S BAKED MACARONI

INGREDIENTS

- 1/2 box Mrs. Mueller's elbow macaroni
- 16 oz. can Del Monte tomato sauce
- 4 Tbs. salted butter, plus extra for buttering dish
- 6 slices Kraft American cheese

DIRECTIONS

Preheat the oven to 375°. Boil the macaroni in water in a medium pot until *al dente* (about 7–8 minutes). Butter the insides of a small casserole dish. Drain the elbows and put them in a bowl. Add the butter and tomato sauce and mix well. Pour into the casserole and cover with the cheese. Bake until the cheese is light brown and serve immediately.

SERVES 3-4—*OR JUST ME!*

Nana's "potted meat" is without a doubt the most delicious brisket recipe you will ever eat! Everyone who has eaten it agrees that its combination of sweet and sour barbeque-like sauce and tender, unctuous meat is outstanding. Once you have made it this way, you will never try another recipe. I have embellished it with the addition of the wine and bay leaf to add some layers of flavor, but it is very close to the original. Our family considers it the ultimate Jewish comfort food, and I serve it at almost all family get-togethers, especially at Hanukkah, as it goes so well with potato *latkes*.

NANA'S POTTED MEAT

INGREDIENTS

1 Tbs. vegetable oil

4–5 lb. beef brisket (1st or thin cut), trimmed of extra but not all fat

3 large onions, halved and sliced

1 cup Heinz ketchup, or more as needed

1/2 cup Manischewitz, or other sweet wine

1 bay leaf

DIRECTIONS

Preheat oven to 350°. Heat the oil over moderate heat in a large, ovenproof casserole. Carefully add the meat, fat side down. While the meat is searing, slice the onions. When the bottom of the meat has browned, use a pair of tongs to turn it over. Once the second side has browned, cover the meat with the onions. Pour the ketchup over the onions to cover them nearly completely. Place the bay leaf on top and pour enough wine to cover the bottom of the pan.

Cover the pot and place in the oven for 2 hours, checking to be sure that it is at a low simmer. After the first hour, carefully turn the meat over, adding more liquid if dry. At the end of the cooking time, remove the pan from the oven, but leave the oven on. Remove the meat to a cutting board and allow to cool for a few minutes. When possible, slice the meat against the grain and return to the pot. Add more wine if the bottom of the pan looks dry. Replace into the oven and cook for another half an hour. This recipe can be made several days in advance or frozen.
SERVES 4-6

Nana was born in Bresla-Tovsk, in what was then Prussia. She came to America around 1903, at the age of five. She was taught that to be a good American, she should not speak Yiddish or Jewish, as she called it, but only English.

She married my grandfather, whom we called Papa, when she was an "old maid" at the age of twenty-eight, which was really was a bit on the late side to marry in those days. That he was younger than she, if by only three months, was a great source of embarrassment for her all her life.

Just as she had been taught as a young girl, she made delicious food using American brand-names but with a nod to her Jewish heritage. She did not eat pork, but she was not too fussy about it. For instance, she loved Chinese egg rolls, and when we told her that they contained roast pork, she argued that they did not. Then she poked at it with her fork, picking out the little pink pieces—but nonetheless, she ate it.

Nana always had some Bazooka bubble gum in her handbag to amuse any restless grandchildren. As American as she was, the one very American food that Nana would not eat was watermelon. My brother, Owen, and I always made fun of her for that. She found it too messy, and the idea of having to spit out the pits was completely beneath her. I especially loved spitting them out in the grass as far as I could spit, which was so unladylike of me—*disgraceful!*

Nana never allowed my mother in the kitchen to cook, fearing the unsightly mess that would surely follow. As a result of this, my mother's style in the kitchen, as well as in everything else, is very precise—making as little mess as possible. I believe that this is why she excelled in baking. My mother was always certain to have the exact ingredients needed for her recipe. I am not given to precision, and so I do not do the amount of baking I did as a child—to say nothing of the extra pounds I would be carrying around my waist if I did.

My mother and I spent many sweet hours together making cookies for company. It always surprises me that parents think they can make cookies with their children, as most cookies require an inordinate amount of precision and patience that no child of mine ever exhibited! Truth be told, my daughter really does enjoy baking and would certainly do more if given the time required. She and her grandmother have some very interesting similarities; precision and patience are definitely traits that went from my mother to my daughter, skipping me!

These cookies were developed by Nana from the Old Country recipe. I have the hand-written original! They are double-baked in the same way that Italian biscotti are prepared and are definitely related to them. I believe that this technique was developed in order to help them stay fresh for weeks. They are delicious dunked in a cup of coffee for a quick breakfast or with a cup of hot tea in the late afternoon. They are called *Mandel Brot*, which means almond bread in Yiddish, but mysteriously, my grandmother always made them with walnuts.

WALNUT MANDEL BROT COOKIES

INGREDIENTS

1/2 cup peanut or vegetable oil
3/4 cup white sugar
1 tsp. almond extract
2 eggs, slightly beaten
2 cups sifted all-purpose flour
Pinch of salt
1 Tbs. baking powder
1 cup walnuts

DIRECTIONS

Preheat oven to 375°. Mix the oil, sugar, and extract until smooth. Add the eggs and combine. In a small bowl, combine the flour, salt, and baking powder. Add this mixture to the first one and mix thoroughly, then add the nuts. Pour into an oblong shape on a cookie sheet. Bake for 30 minutes. Cool slightly and then cut in to 3/4-inch slices. Place slices on their sides and bake for another 10 minutes or so, until lightly toasted.

YIELDS ABOUT 15–20 COOKIES

My father had a very hard time sticking to a recipe; he clearly must have thought it would be boring beyond belief. He much preferred to wing it! Of course, when you are precise like my mom, you are assured perfection every time, while winging it can produce failure as well as success. For him, as well as for me, that was part of the fun, because you never know what to expect! My dad was the "throw in some of this and that" style, which in Yiddish is called *shitereyne*. This was his mother's style of cooking as well. Whenever I asked Bubbe how to prepare something, she answered, "shitereyne," which always made me laugh!!

This style is not suited for the precise needs of baking, so my dad preferred cooking over baking. He unfortunately had the distressing habit of using every pot, pan, dish, and utensil available whenever he cooked, leaving a hurricane of dishes in the sink. He always threw his whole being into the process and "to hell with the mess"! I suppose it helped that he had full-time cleaning help!

Bubbe and Zeyda

My dad grew up in a kosher home in the Bronx in the 1930s. My father's mother, Bubbe, as we called her, was quite a character. She was born in Austria and came to the Lower East Side of New York around 1915. Her mother, Fryma Sarah, arrived at Ellis Island widowed with six children and one on the way. She had about forty dollars in her pocket and started a little dress business by renting a rack in her cousin's dress store and filling it with her designs. She managed to raise the children on her own by living a very frugal life. I have a copy of her handwritten will, which states that she never went to the movies and never had a happy day in her life.

Bubbe's nickname when she was a child, was "big-eyes," because she eyed the eggs on her brothers' plates jealously while she and the other girls in the family were given none. That is how poor they were! However, Fryma Sarah instilled in my grandmother the devotion to family and traditional Jewish culture that were at the very core of her being.

Eastern European Jewish cuisine separates meat and milk along with dozens of other mandates for keeping kosher. This region of Jewish cuisine has a big emphasis on a sweet and sour taste. You will find this taste combination in borscht, stuffed cabbage, and my favorite—chicken fricassee. My grandmother was an ambitious, yet not always successful, cook. In the same way that I succeed in cooking but am less successful in the baking department, her savory dishes were always spot-on! She took great pleasure in cooking for her family, and this dish was one I always loved and still do. I received the written version of this recipe from my Aunt Blanche, her daughter.

Chicken fricassee, with its deceiving name that sounds very French, was made with the least expensive meat: ground beef, chicken wings, and *pupiks*. Bubbe told my brother, Owen, and me that *pupiks* were the chickens' belly buttons. We found the idea hilarious! But they are in fact, the gizzards; I cannot bring myself to include them in my version. This dish tastes really good the first day, and even better the next day. I often serve them as an appetizer to the Passover Seder meal.

CHICKEN FRICASSEE

INGREDIENTS

Meatballs

1 lb. ground beef
1 egg, beaten
2 celery stalks, shredded
1 onion, shredded
1/4 cup matzo meal
1/2 tsp. salt
1/4 tsp. black pepper

----

2 Tbs. vegetable oil
3–4 lbs. chicken wings, cut in
   pieces
1 large onion, chopped

Sauce

4 cups tomato sauce
2 cups water (or more)
2 carrots, sliced
1 green pepper, cut in 1-inch
   pieces
2 garlic cloves, chopped
1/4 cup raisins
1/4 cup brown sugar
1 tsp. sour salt or juice of 1
   lemon
2 tsp. salt
1/2 tsp. black pepper

DIRECTIONS

To make the meatballs, squeeze the onion and celery in a dishcloth to remove excess moisture and then combine with the remaining ingredients, up to the black pepper. Roll the meat balls into marble-sized balls. Heat the oil in a large pot and add the chicken and onions and sauté until lightly brown. Add the tomato sauce and bring to a simmer. Add the meatballs, water, carrots, green pepper, garlic and raisins. Bring to a simmer, cover, and cook over a low heat for about 20 minutes. Add the raisins and remaining ingredients, and cover and cook another 20 minutes. If possible, refrigerate overnight before reheating.

SERVES 4–6

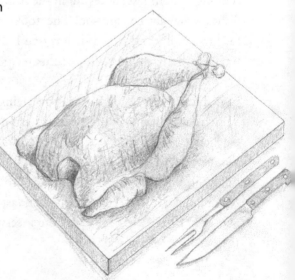

Stuffed cabbage was one of Bubbe's best dishes. It combines the sweet and sour taste that is so popular in Eastern European Jewish dishes, and it is very economical, which was necessary in the Jewish *shtetls* (ghettos) of Poland and Austria in the early twentieth century. Every family had a small garden and grew cabbages. With one small pound of ground beef, a large feast could be made. Bubbe called her stuffed cabbage, *cholupszes*.

My Polish daughter-in-law, Roza, and I made Bubbe's stuffed cabbage one day, and although it brought me back to Bubbe's table, it was not what Roza remembered from her grandmother. It seems that the whole sweet and sour thing is not part of non-Jewish Polish cuisine. Roza has taught me that stuffed cabbage in Polish is *galumpki* and the word for grandmother is *babcia*. I know she enjoyed the process, and next time I will have her make her babcia's version.

Some years ago, Roza and my middle son, Zach, were married in a traditional Polish wedding ceremony in the small village of Shetlev in western Poland. Just as I knew it would be, galumpkis were served at the lavish wedding banquet and again at the feast of leftovers the next day. They were not my Bubbe's stuffed cabbage but they were very delicious, and of course, they were even better the next day!

STUFFED CABBAGE

INGREDIENTS

1 large cabbage, cored and boiled until tender, about 30 minutes

1 beef bone, with meat and marrow

1 tsp. olive oil

28 oz. can chopped tomatoes

16 oz. can tomato sauce

1/2 cup catsup

2 large onions, sliced

1 green pepper, diced

1 carrot, diced

1/4 cup raisins

1/3 cup brown sugar (or more, to taste)

1 tsp. sour salt (or more, to taste)

1/2 tsp. garlic powder

1 lb. ground beef

1/2 cup medium-grain white rice

1 onion, chopped and sautéed in 1 Tbs. olive oil

2 eggs, beaten

1/4 cup catsup

2 garlic cloves, chopped

1/2 tsp. paprika

2 tsp. kosher salt

1 1/2 tsp. pepper

1/2 cup sauerkraut

DIRECTIONS

Prepare the sauce by first browning the bone in the oil. Add the tomatoes, tomato sauce, catsup, pepper, carrot, raisins, salt, and pepper. Simmer for half an hour, then add the sour salt and brown sugar. Taste for a nice balance of sweet and sour. While the sauce is starting to simmer, prepare the stuffing. Combine the ground beef, rice, sautéed onions, eggs, catsup, garlic, paprika, salt, and pepper. Mix until combined. Preheat the oven to 400°. Peel off one layer of cabbage at a time and slice off any tough ribs. Place 1 Tbs. of filling into the center of the leaf and roll up, tucking in the sides as you go. After you have prepared all the cabbage rolls, roll any leftover stuffing into meatballs. Carefully lower the cabbage rolls (and any meatballs) into a wide baking dish and pour the sauce over them. Tuck the sauerkraut into whatever space is available. Cover with aluminum foil and bake for an hour or so. This dish tastes even better when prepared one day in advance; it freezes very well too.

SERVES 6–8

Bubbe was a fierce woman, fifty years before Tyra Banks made it popular for women to be fierce. She did everything with great passion—almost with a vengeance. She loved her children and grandchildren with the love of a wild animal ready to defend her young at any moment. My father often spoke of the time when he came home from school in the Bronx at age eight with a bloody nose, having been punched by a bigger boy. My grandmother insisted that he point out the boy who had done this and then she proceeded to pin the boy's arms behind his back and insisted that my father hit the boy in the face. He was never bothered by him again. It is hard to imagine anyone I know doing this today!

Bubbe embodied the Yiddish term, *balabusta,* which literally means hard-working housewife. She cooked with the same intensity that she did everything. My dad said that when he was growing up, she would prepare three-course meals every night of the week. I think that she was very proud to have enough money to make a fine meal every night because she grew up with literally next to nothing.

American products or processed food were rare items in her kitchen. She was not a fine baker, but Bubbe made all the cookies, cakes, breads, and crackers that she served. The honest truth is that I dreaded the boxes of homemade cookies and cakes that Bubbe would send up to New York from Miami because they always tasted stale and were as dry as dust. When she would ask me how everything tasted, I would have to lie and tell her it was all so delicious. And because we "enjoyed" it all so much she would set about making the next new box of treats for us!

One of my favorite baked items that she made (when they were fresh out of the oven) were the savory homemade crackers called *tzibbole pletzels,* which means onion crackers. I don't understand why we don't make crackers any more. They are so quick to make and everyone is always so impressed when you say you made the crackers yourself. These are an unusual and old-time treat that are great on their own or served with chopped liver or eggplant salad.

BUBBE'S TZIBBOLE PLETZELS

INGREDIENTS

4 cups flour

2 eggs

2 heaping teaspoons baking
  powder

1 Tbs. kosher salt

Work together with hands to
  form dough.

Then add:

3/4 cup vegetable oil

1/2 cup water

2 Tbs. poppy seeds

3 small onions, diced

DIRECTIONS

Mix thoroughly and roll out to 1/4-inch thick and cut into circles with biscuit cutter. Lightly grease pan and bake at 375° for about 25 minutes. Serve soon after baking or put into tins.

When my father was growing up, he loved his mother's apple *strudel*. Every girl in Austria, where Bubbe grew up, was taught to make strudel. She made the classic apple strudel: not too sweet, with fresh apple, sweet butter, and cinnamon in a flaky, rolled, home-made strudel dough. Strudel means *whirlpool* in German, which is the shape the dough takes as you roll it around the apple filling. I recently made my own strudel dough with my son Toby's girl-friend, Brittany, and it was an extremely satisfying experience. The dough was soft and pliable, and I was easily able to stretch it so thin that you could actually see the design of the tablecloth over which I stretched the dough.

Because my father told his mother that he loved her apple stru-del, she was inspired to make it even better by adding raisins—and then, because she had a prolific mango tree in Miami Beach, she added mangoes. The final addition was coconut, and then my father called it Super Strudel, and he no longer liked it. However, he knew better than to say that to her!

APPLE STRUDEL

INGREDIENTS

6 large apples, any variety
6 sheets phyllo pastry
1 stick unsalted butter
2 Tbs. white sugar
1 Tbs. ground cinnamon
1 tsp. lemon juice
Whipped cream or ice cream,
    optional

DIRECTIONS

Preheat the oven to 350°. Core, peel, and thinly slice the apples. Melt 3 Tbs. of the butter in a sauté pan. Add the apples and sauté over medium heat until the apples soften and begin to caramelize. Add 1-1/2 tablespoons of the sugar and 1/2 tablespoon of the cinnamon. Cook for another 5 minutes, turn off the heat, and mix in the lemon juice. Melt the remaining butter. While the apples cool, take the phyllo dough out of the package and wrap it completely in plastic.

Using a plastic place mat as a working surface, unroll the phyllo and take 1 sheet and place it on your work surface. Immediately reroll the rest of the phyllo in the plastic. Quickly paint the entire surface of the dough with the melted butter, using a pastry brush. Unroll the phyllo again and place another sheet on top of the first. Be sure to rewrap the dough in the plastic each time to prevent it from drying out. Repeat the process until you have 6 layers.

Place the apples in a line along one of the short ends of the dough and roll it up as tightly as possible. Paint with the melted butter. Sprinkle the top with the remaining sugar and cinnamon.

Place on a greased cookie sheet and bake for about 30 minutes or until golden brown. Serve warm with whipped cream or ice cream, if desired.
SERVES 4–6

Bubbe loved her little house in Miami Beach. Her living room and dining room were crammed with the very heavy European furniture that was brought over from the Old Country. She had twin beds in the master bedroom (where I slept next to her), a guest room (where my brother slept), a compact kitchen, a Florida room (which we would call a den), and the best place of all—a garden in the backyard.

Her yard could not have been more than eight hundred square feet, but she grew every type of tropical fruit imaginable. She grew mangoes; bananas; tiny, sour calamondin oranges; pineapples; and guava—but most of all, she grew grapefruit. She had only one tree, but this tree could produce! She told me that her secret was putting coffee grounds on the soil every day, and it must have worked!

One winter we drove down in the Lincoln Continental and entirely filled the trunk with grapefruits, probably over two hundred of them rolling around in the trunk from Miami to Long Island, and then we ate them every day for many months. My father's favorite breakfast specialty was broiled grapefruit. We considered it to be very gourmet whenever he made them, which was mostly on Sundays. My tongue hurts just thinking about those burning hot grapefruits!

BROILED GRAPEFRUIT

INGREDIENTS

2 grapefruits, halved crosswise
2 Tbs. dark brown sugar
1 Tbs. dark rum, optional

DIRECTIONS

Preheat the oven broiler. Section the grapefruits. Sprinkle the grapefruits with the brown sugar and the rum. Put onto a small sheet pan and broil until the sugar has bubbled. Serve warm.

Bubbe's mango tree was so prolific that she needed to sell most of her mangoes to a buyer, who would go through the Miami neighborhoods buying mangoes from private homes. Mangoes were always in season when we came down for Christmas break. Bubbe and I would sit for many hours a day at her kitchen table peeling and slicing mangoes to put into jars for the freezer. They were incredibly juicy and aromatic, unlike any mango you can find in the Northeast. I would eat two for breakfast and two for lunch, and Bubbe was always worried it would upset my belly. I was just fine because it seems that I have always had an iron stomach, and I still do!

One year, my father decided that he would climb up into this enormous tree and pick all the mangoes. What he didn't know was that the mango's stem produces a liquid that is highly allergenic. I suppose this is a defense mechanism that the trees produce to keep predators away. The next night he was awakened by an intensely itchy dermatitis that nearly drove him insane for months. It bothered and worried him a great deal because it seems that this particular dermatitis can be fatal. He ended up getting relief from some very strong medication that he needed to take any time he accidentally ate some mango.

Bubbe's mangoes did not last very long because they were super ripe and needed to be canned, frozen, or prepared within a few days. We were not able to take many home successfully, but the few we managed to take were often made into a scrumptious mango mousse. My cousin Fred, my dad's sister's son, lives in Miami and shares my grandmother's love of gardening. This past summer he mailed me six of his best mangoes. Two of them burst on the way from extreme ripeness, but I relished the remaining four with great delight!

My parents gave enormous themed parties every year, one for business associates and a week later, a second party with the same theme for friends. One year they gave a Caribbean-themed party with curried shrimp, a roast suckling pig, and that scrumptious mango mousse for dessert. They often invited close to a hundred guests, and so the amount of food to be prepared was quite daunting. I was expected to help prepare the food, which I really did love, and I think that is why I felt prepared to start a catering business many years later. One of the guests at the Caribbean party was the wife of the only African-American friends my parents had.

Tina was highly allergic to shrimp, which up until that night was only a problem if she ate them. However, when she walked into our house, which was filled with the fumes of fifteen pounds of shrimp cooking on the stove, she had to go immediately to the emergency room. My father was a physician at the local hospital, so he drove her there, leaving my mother to host the party by herself until his return. It was quite frightening and dramatic, and unfortunately, it was the last time my parents saw EG and Tina.

Despite the misfortune of the shrimp episode, the party was a lot of fun and ended with the incredible mango mousse. Many, many years later, I taught this recipe to my dear friend Gili's unusually gifted daughter, Shai. Shai is now a Registered Nurse, and does not have as much time to cook as she did then, but I know that she still loves it. I had the absolute pleasure of teaching her many recipes. Shai and her family fell in love with this recipe and make it very often when they entertain.

MANGO MOUSSE

INGREDIENTS

5 mangoes
1 lime
2 egg whites
1/3 cup sugar
1/2 cup whipping cream

DIRECTIONS

Cut the mangoes into cubes. Separate 1 cup of mango. Place the rest in a blender and puree. Add the lime juice. Beat the egg whites until stiff. Add the sugar and continue to beat the egg whites for a few more minutes. In a separate bowl, beat the cream until thick. Fold 1/2 cup of the mango puree into the egg whites, then fold the cream, puree, and mango pieces into the egg whites. Pour into a large bowl and refrigerate for at least 4 hours.
SERVES 6–8

While in high school in the Bronx, my father earned a swimming scholarship for college in Louisiana. His scholarship was to Tulane University; however, when he and my grandmother arrived in New Orleans to move him into the boarding house, the woman who owned the house asked my grandmother which church Billy was going to attend on Sunday. Bubbe replied that Billy was not going to go to church on Sunday; rather, he would go to the synagogue on Saturday. At this, the woman responded that the room she thought she had was no longer available.

My father then called Louisiana State University, which had also offered him a full swimming scholarship, and they headed over to Baton Rouge. The only room available was a room in the stadium next to the LSU mascot—a live tiger! My dad said it took him a very long time to get used to the smell and the noise from his next-door neighbor. I know this sounds impossible, but it really happened!

Moving from a kosher home in the Bronx to a suburb of the Big Easy was a huge culture shock for my dad, but he relished every minute of the experience. The change from traditional kosher Jewish food to New Orleans Cajun/Creole cuisine was life-altering, and he brought his love of this adopted culture back with him and expanded his love of food from that moment on. He told me that his palate had been so "deprived" that he had never even tasted an olive until he went to college and that my grandmother did not even own a pepper shaker.

He had a true dramatic flair and always enjoyed preparing food in front of his guests. One of his favorite and tastiest shows was to flambé crêpes in his famous Crêpes Suzette. He learned this recipe from the chef at one of the most famous restaurants in New Orleans, Brennan's, and it was quite the show! The sauce is sweet yet tangy, elegant and sophisticated; it was the stuff of my dreams.

BILL KALT'S CRÊPES SUZETTE

INGREDIENTS

6 Tbs. white sugar

1 stick unsalted butter

3 oranges—zested, juiced, and quartered

2 lemons—zested, juiced, and quartered

1 can frozen orange juice, thawed

1 oz. Cointreau or Grand Marnier

1 oz. brandy

8–10 crêpes, homemade or store-bought

DIRECTIONS

Melt the sugar in a large sauté pan over medium heat, but do not let it brown. Add the butter and simmer until blended. Add the juices, zest, and quartered fruit and cook over medium heat until thickened. Allow to simmer for about half an hour. Add the Cointreau or Grand Marnier and simmer for a few minutes. Pour over the warmed crêpes. Warm the brandy and then light it with a match as you pour it over the crêpes.

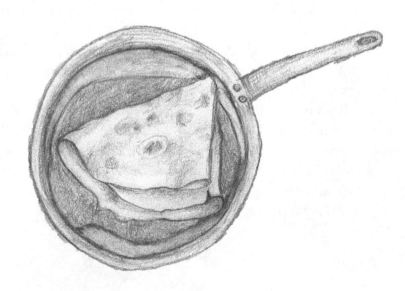

According to my dad, Bubbe made soup almost every evening. She served three or four courses for a weekday supper, and usually soup was one of them. She made chicken soup with matzo balls, cold beet borscht in the summer, and hot beef borscht in the winter. She made *schav*, which was made from sorrel or spinach. My dad's favorite soup that Bubbe made for him was *knoble* borscht with *chipkele*, which translates as garlic borsht with potato dumplings. I remember having it only once, but dad talked about it all the time.

Bubbe definitely ruled the kitchen, but she was married to Leo, whom we called Zeyda, and he most definitely ruled the rest of the house and often way beyond! He came to America from Austria as a youngster, but it took seven crossings of the Atlantic as a cabin boy before he was permitted to leave the boat. He could not afford the price of the voyage, so he was indentured as a cabin boy until the captain determined that he had paid his way.

When Zeyda married Bubbe in New York, he joined the garment business with her family and opened a small dress shop in Brooklyn. They stayed there until he had a heart attack when he was in his fifties, and then they moved to Miami Beach. He eventually opened a dress factory in Miami, which I visited as a young girl. I remember seeing him come towards me in the factory, and he was so happy to see me that he twirled me around and around.

For some mysterious and terrible reason, Zeyda did not want my father to marry my mother, and before their wedding he called the whole family and threatened that if any of them attended my parents' wedding, he would disown them from the family. Unfortunately, they all listened to him, and not a soul from my father's family came to their wedding. My parents did not see or speak to Bubbe and Zeyda from that moment on until I was born.

As a result of this and the fact that they lived in Florida, we saw them very seldom, and Zeyda died when I was eight years old from his third heart attack. He had a red-headed temper, and he and Bubbe had a very stormy marriage, which may explain why he is buried in New York and she in Miami.

To get back to the subject of soup; there are many kinds of borscht: hot, cold, Russian, Polish, and Ukrainian. There is borscht with only beets as well as borscht with all kinds of meat and any vegetable that happens to be hiding in the back of the vegetable bin. Bubbe's borscht was called *knuble* borscht because of the amount of garlic (knuble) in it. The predominant taste in Bubbe's version of the soup is classic Eastern European Jewish. It has a distinctly sweet and sour taste that requires a real balance of brown sugar and sour salt or lemon juice.

As diverse as the ingredients for the soup are, so are the garnishes: sour cream (which Bubbe would never use in the beef version as it mixed meat and dairy, a kosher no-no), a boiled potato, a sprinkling of fresh dill or parsley. I recently tasted my son Adam's version of borscht, which deliciously contained a lot of smoked bacon. Bubbe would definitely not have eaten it, but we all licked the bowls clean.

Mom and Dad, June 1952

NOT BUBBE'S BEEF AND VEGETABLE BORSCHT

INGREDIENTS

2 lbs. soup beef (flanken, shin, ribs, or brisket)
2 lbs. beef bones
1 onion, diced
1 Tbs. vegetable oil
8 cups water
3 beets—washed, unpeeled, and trimmed with 1 inch of stems left on
5 new potatoes, unpeeled and cubed
1 celery stalk, sliced
1 parsnip, peeled and sliced
1 carrot, peeled and sliced
1/2 green pepper, cubed
1/2 red pepper, cubed
1 28 oz. can chopped-tomatoes or 3 large fresh tomatoes, cubed
1 small cabbage, thinly sliced
2 cloves garlic, sliced
2 dill and parsley sprigs
3 Tbs. brown sugar (or more, to taste)
1 tsp. sour salt (citric acid) or 1 Tbs. lemon juice (or more, to taste)
Salt and pepper, to taste

DIRECTIONS

Sauté the meat, bones, and onion in the oil until lightly browned. Cover with water; add more water if needed to cover the meat. Add the beets. Bring to a boil, skimming off any foam that surfaces. Simmer for one hour. Remove beets and allow to cool. Rub the skin off the beets and slice them. Add all the vegetables and 1 sprig of dill, and simmer for 1 hour. Add the brown sugar, sour salt (or lemon juice) and salt and pepper. Simmer for half an hour and taste for extra seasoning. Remove meat and bones. Dice meat and return to pot, adding more water if necessary. Refrigerate overnight if possible and remove any fat on surface of soup. Reheat, taste for seasoning, and garnish with remaining dill. This soup freezes very well.

SERVES 4–6

When I was six years old, we packed up all our things (I was in charge of packing my toys, and I am quite sure I simply tossed everything, broken crayons and all, into boxes), and we left that sweet little house in Wantagh. I was hoping that all my friends on the street would be there waving goodbye as we drove off, but that didn't happen. I suppose that no one knew we were leaving at that moment, and so it was a very sad and quiet farewell.

I was, however, excited that we were moving to a big house with a big yard, but I think I knew that the fancy neighborhood we were moving to could never offer a six-year-old the joys of neighborhood kids, playgrounds, and the pride that sidewalks offered to small children off to visit their friends independently. I certainly never had that freedom again until I learned to drive.

Me, 1960

CHAPTER 2

5 SYCAMORE DRIVE
WOODBURY, NEW YORK
1960-1974

We moved from the tiny, sweet house in Wantagh to a sprawling showcase of a home in Woodbury when I was six years old. The home supposedly had been owned by a "mobster" and therefore had a very glitzy look, which was very appealing to my up-and-coming parents. It was a ranch house with a very contemporary feel, and the entry-way was covered in metallic silver and gold wallpaper. There were two steps down to the living room, marble floors in the den, and a huge eat-in kitchen overlooking an expansive backyard. In the kitchen there were large bay windows surrounding the breakfast table. These kitchen windows were my first view into nature and its beauty.

The windows looked out onto a great hill for sledding, and at the top of the hill were woods for exploring, and next door was my sometime best friend, Linda Friedlander. Linda's mother was a concentration camp survivor from Hungary. Her name was Henny, and she loved to cook and to feed everyone who came to her home. She grew her own vegetables, especially peppers, as she was a true

Hungarian. I still feel guilty for having stolen some of the most delicious peppers I have ever eaten from her garden. She taught me to eat things I never would have tried at home. The most unusual dish she introduced me to was lamb bone marrow, and this was decades before it was all the rage. I loved the soft, fatty, unctuousness of it from my first taste, and it is still one of my favorite treats. I think of her every time I enjoy marrow.

Green peppers have never tasted as good to me as those peppers stolen from Henny's garden—except for my Uncle Nat's pickled peppers. Uncle Nat was my father's first cousin and was a very sweet man who towered over all of us. He and his wife, Ruth, had three sons, each of whom is well over six feet tall. My father was at one time on par with them. Sitting in a room surrounded by all these skyscrapers was quite intimidating for me; I am not even five feet in heels.

Nat was a great gardener and a wonderful cook. Almost every member of my father's family has great interest and really great talent in the kitchen, and Uncle Nat was no exception. He was also known as Big Nat, so as not to be confused with Little Natie, another uncle. I remember very fondly sitting at his dining room table enjoying the many dishes he prepared from the vegetables he had grown in his garden. Aside from gardening and cooking, Nat truly loved watching his family and friends eagerly devour his creations. His pickled peppers were not to be missed. They are very similar to the almost as delicious ones served at Famous Sammy's Roumanian Steakhouse in New York City, a perennial favorite in our household to this day.

UNCLE NAT'S PICKLED PEPPERS

INGREDIENTS

3 lbs. red and/or green Bell peppers
6 cloves garlic, peeled and sliced
2 Tbs. vegetable oil
2 tsp. salt
3 Tbs. sugar
3 Tbs. water
2 cups white vinegar

DIRECTIONS

Char the peppers on the grill, on top of a gas stove, or under the broiler until the skin is nearly black all over. Place the peppers in a large glass bowl and cover with plastic wrap and allow to cool. When cool enough to handle, peel them, but leave the peppers whole. Layer the peppers in the bottom of a glass jar with a tightly sealed lid. Be sure that the jar is large enough to hold all the ingredients. Add all the other ingredients to the jar and seal tightly. Marinate in the refrigerator for two days. (Will keep in the refrigerator for about 2 weeks.)

SERVES 4–6 AS A SIDE DISH

Of all the great cooks in my father's family, only one ever cooked outside the home, and he developed quite a name for himself. That is my second cousin, Stephen Kalt. Stephen owned several restaurants in Manhattan, including Spartina, which was located very close to the Twin Towers and suffered the fate of many businesses in that area. We ate at Spartina when my oldest son, Adam, turned thirteen and was already an enthusiastic diner. The curious thing we discovered was that he and Stephen share the same birthday, and the day that Adam turned thirteen and we celebrated at Spartina, Stephen turned forty. The last time I had seen Stephen was at a family Bar Mitzvah when we both were thirteen.

When we visited Spartina, it had just been reviewed in *New York Magazine* by Mimi Sheraton, and the title of the article was "Lamb Shank Redemption." Stephen's slow-cooked lamb shanks were featured in the article and really led the way in the Slow Food movement. I saw him in the early days on The Food Network on *Iron Chef America* and recently on *Beat Bobby Flay*. It has been very exciting watching his career. As you can see, he and my dad have a strong family resemblance.

Dad   Stephen

Although Big Nat and Stephen lived in New York, the rest of my father's family lived and still reside in Miami, so we did not spend all that much time together growing up. However, now I try to visit with my cousin Fred in Miami or New York at least once a year. One summer, we met in Montreal, which was a real treat.

On the other hand, my mother's family lived right nearby all through my childhood. Nana and Papa lived half an hour away in an apartment in Hempstead, Long Island. It was very exciting for me to push the elevator button to their floor and go out to lunch later with Nana at the luncheonette across the street. Every time I visited, we went there, and every time we went there, I ordered the same thing. I would have a hamburger (cheese on the burger was forbidden by my kosher grandmother) and a cherry-Coke. I loved sitting on the stool at the counter and spinning and spinning until Nana couldn't bear it any longer, and we moved to a booth.

My mother's sister, Roda, lived right up the street from us in Wantagh, and when we moved to Woodbury, they moved to Woodbury as well. You would think that this meant they were very close, but on the contrary, they could not tolerate each other. Roda and her husband, Gil, who was an internist, worked at the same hospital as my father. They had two daughters, Cary and Nina, who are three and two years older than I.

I was so lucky to have them in my school with me. They introduced me to folk music—Judy Collins, Joni Mitchell, and Bob Dylan. I don't know if I ever would have discovered all of my favorite musicians without them. I got all their hand-me-downs, which did not feel so lucky at the time, but it felt as if I were their younger sister. I am still very close to them and treasure them as my family.

Roda did not enjoy cooking so much, but she made a nice effort on our occasional meals at their home. One Thanksgiving, Roda served a Ritz Cracker stuffing that was the most delicious food I had ever tasted. It is a very simple, bare-bones kind of recipe, which works very well with roast chicken or turkey.

Nina, Cary, Mom, and me, 1960

AUNT RODA'S RITZ CRACKER STUFFING

INGREDIENTS

4 large Bermuda-type onions, diced

3 Tbs. unsalted butter

2 boxes Ritz Crackers, crushed

2 cups chicken broth

DIRECTIONS

Preheat the oven to 350°. Sauté the onions in a large pan over moderate heat until they soften and become translucent. Place in a large bowl and add the crushed crackers. Sprinkle with broth, but do not let it get mushy. Place in a greased casserole dish and bake 1 hour or until browned.

SERVES 6

Gil was on a very strict diet, having suffered a heart attack in his early sixties. He came for dinner one night when I had prepared ratatouille. I had pretty much just thrown all the season's vegetables and every herb I could find in the cabinet into a large pot—and, *Voila!* I first discovered this dish as a teenager at a crêpe restaurant in Manhattan. Every time I went to this place, I ordered the crêpes with ratatouille.

I decided to try to repeat the dish at home—and with great results. Gil raved so much about my ratatouille that for the first time in my young life, I understood that I had some talent in the kitchen. His compliments touched me so much because I knew that he truly meant what he said. Every time I make this dish, I think of him, and it reminds me how much our words can mean to young people who have a passion for something.

My parents had a very small garden, which was maintained entirely by our housekeeper, Anna. As it was the end of summer, there were tomatoes, eggplants, zucchini, peppers—just about everything you need for ratatouille. (As much as I love my own garden, I am really never too sad to see the gardening season come to an end, because at this point in the season I have lost most of my interest in weeding and caring for it.) Luckily, the fruits of my labor were all on the vine, ready to be picked and made into ratatouille.

RATATOUILLE

INGREDIENTS

3 Tbs. extra-virgin olive oil

1 large eggplant, peeled and cut into 2-inch pieces

1/2 cup shallots, peeled and cut in half

3 garlic cloves, sliced

2 large zucchini, cut into thick circles

1 large yellow squash, cut into thick circles

1 large green pepper, cut into 2-inch pieces

1 large red pepper, cut into 2-inch pieces

6 fresh tomatoes, chopped— or 2 cups canned plum tomatoes

1 handful fresh basil, torn into small pieces

1 bay leaf

1 tsp. dried or fresh oregano

1 tsp. dried marjoram

1/2 tsp. dried tarragon

Salt and pepper, to taste

DIRECTIONS

Cut all the vegetables into 2-inch pieces. Heat a large pan with a cover over moderate heat. Add half the olive oil. When the oil is hot, add the eggplant, stir for a few minutes, add the shallots and garlic, and cook for a few more minutes. Add the zucchini, squash, and peppers—and cook for a few more minutes. Add the tomatoes and seasonings to the vegetables and sprinkle in the salt and pepper. Then cook for another 10 minutes. Taste for seasoning.

SERVES 4–6

My parents traveled often and had the luxury of my grand-parents nearby to babysit while they were away. Nana gave me the structure and rules that I didn't have from my parents. I didn't resent her for this because I believe that children crave limits, and I knew that they came from a place of love and concern—as some might say, "worry"! She was the perfect grandmother, and I treasure the time we had together.

While my parents were in Mexico, they tasted Mexican choco-late and brought some home to me. I had never had the combination of chocolate and cinnamon, and it seemed so exotic at the time. Soon after their trip to Mexico, my parents threw an extravagant party with a Mexican theme and served these scrumptious choco-late cupcakes. They are deceptively simple to prepare but incredibly moist and fragrant.

Nana and Papa, 1974

MEXICAN CHOCOLATE CUPCAKES

INGREDIENTS

1 3/4 cups sifted cake flour

1 Tbs. baking powder

1/4 tsp. sea salt

1 tsp. ground cinnamon

1/4 tsp. ground cloves

2 oz. bittersweet chocolate, melted in a double boiler

5 Tbs. boiling water

1/2 cup unsalted butter, softened

1 cup white sugar

4 eggs, separated

1/2 cup whole milk

1 tsp. vanilla extract

1 Tbs. confectioner's sugar combined with 1 Tbs. unsweetened cocoa

DIRECTIONS

Preheat the oven to 350°. Place paper liners into two 12-cupcake pans. Sift the flour with the baking powder, salt, cinnamon, and cloves into a medium bowl. Add the boiling water to the melted chocolate. In a small bowl, cream the butter and the sugar, then add the egg yolks one at a time, beating well after each yolk. Add the chocolate and then add this and the milk alternately in three parts to the flour mixture. Add the vanilla. Beat the egg whites until stiff and then fold into the batter. Fill the cupcake liners halfway and bake for 10–12 minutes, or until a toothpick comes up dry when poked into the center. Allow to cool and then sprinkle with the confectioner's sugar/ cocoa mixture.

YIELD: 24 CUPCAKES

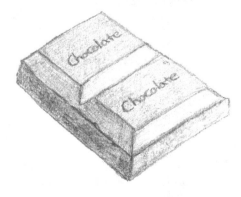

On the topic of chocolate and cinnamon, one of the earliest recipes I remember preparing was a snack that I invented at a friend's house. We were hungry after coming home from elementary school, and there was nothing to eat. Sue and I came up with something we called Chocolate Cinnamon Toast. It was one of those guilty pleasures that, at age nine, was exactly what I was craving. I would definitely find it too sweet today, but I think it was my first kitchen creation.

CHOCOLATE CINNAMON TOAST

INGREDIENTS

1/2 stick unsalted butter
1/4 cup white sugar
1/4 cup unsweetened cocoa
1 tsp. ground cinnamon
6 slices white toast

DIRECTIONS

Melt the butter in a small saucepan over low heat and then add the sugar, mixing until the sugar melts. Add the cocoa and the cinnamon and spread on the toast.

I began cooking for school projects when I was in fifth or sixth grade. The first recipe I remember preparing in front of an audience was for chocolate-covered donuts. I suppose I must have brought a small deep fryer with me. I do remember flipping the donuts in the hot oil and then brushing them with a chocolate glaze. I surely must have been intimidated by the splashing oil, but I managed to cook and serve them. I have no idea what lesson, if any, they were related to. All I remember is that they were finished in a flash! This recipe uses a donut pan, not a deep-fat fryer, eliminating intimidation.

CHOCOLATE-COVERED DONUTS

INGREDIENTS

1 cup all-purpose flour
1 tsp. baking powder
1/4 tsp. baking soda
1 large egg
1/2 cup packed light-brown sugar
1/4 cup whole milk
1/4 cup plain yogurt
2 Tbs. unsalted butter, melted
1 1/2 tsp. vanilla extract
1/2 cup semisweet chocolate chips
2 Tbs. unsalted butter
2 tsp. light corn syrup
2 tsp. water

DIRECTIONS

Preheat the oven to 350°. Coat a standard-sized donut-pan with nonstick cooking spray. Set aside. In a medium bowl—whisk flour, baking powder, and baking soda. In a separate medium bowl—whisk egg, brown sugar, milk, yogurt, butter, and vanilla until smooth. Stir wet ingredients into dry ingredients, just until combined. Pipe the batter into donut cavities with a piping bag and bake for 8–10 minutes, until donuts are golden and spring back to the touch. Allow donuts to slightly cool before glazing. In a medium pan, combine chocolate chips, butter, corn syrup, and water and cook over medium heat, stirring constantly until melted. Pour into a shallow pie pan. Dip donut tops into the chocolate glaze.

What I do remember very clearly and with some embarrassment was the hummus I made in a blender in my sixth-grade class. We were studying Ancient Egypt, and I thought it would be a big hit to prepare a typically Middle Eastern dish. I still remember the off-putting smell of the canned chickpeas as I poured them into the blender; I was really nauseated. I am quite sure that only my teacher tasted it, and that I may have *pretended* to enjoy it.

I have learned a few secrets to preparing delicious hummus since then. The key is to soak dried chickpeas and then cook them in a pressure cooker. *Never use canned chickpeas! Don't throw away the water they were cooked in! Remove the outer skin of as many of the chickpeas as possible to achieve the smoothest texture! Don't cool them too long before putting them in the blender! Add plenty of tahini! Add plenty of fresh lemon juice! Enjoy as soon as possible after preparation!* These many rules come from years of trial and error. But honestly, however you make it, it will taste much better than the store-bought variety—unless you are in Israel, where every package of store-bought hummus is incredibly delicious. It is so delicious that I find that I am happily eating hummus in Israel three times a day.

THE BEST HUMMUS

INGREDIENTS

1 2/3 cups dried chickpeas, soaked overnight in water

1 garlic clove, peeled

1 tsp. sea salt

1/2 cup tahini (sesame paste), well-mixed

1/4 cup freshly squeezed lemon juice

3 Tbs. flavorful olive oil

2 tsp. fresh parsley

1/4 tsp. sweet paprika

DIRECTIONS

Drain the chickpeas and put into a medium saucepan and cover with twice as much water. Cook in a pressure cooker for half an hour. Alternatively, bring to a boil over medium high heat and turn down to a simmer. Partially cover and simmer for about 50 minutes, until very tender with the skins starting to come off. Drain well but do not throw away the cooking liquid. Peel the skins off as many as possible and place the chickpeas together with 1/4 cup of the cooking liquid into a food processor or blender. Process for 3–4 minutes, scraping the sides down every now and then. Put into a large bowl. Crush the garlic and salt together in a mortar and pestle and add to the chickpeas. In a small bowl add the tahini and the lemon juice and mix with a fork until light. Add to the chickpea mixture. Taste for additional lemon or salt. Place onto a wide plate and drizzle with the olive oil, parsley, and paprika.

YIELD: 2 1/2 CUPS

Although the hummus incident was embarrassing, I had enough self-esteem to try out for the cheerleading team and was put on as an alternate because I was able to do a Russian split. The truth is that I had never watched a single football game and had absolutely no idea what was going on. I watched my teammates and cheered or booed whenever they did.

Cheerleading in Middle School, 1969

It's funny to think of the many times I cooked for my classmates, never knowing that this would one day be my career, which did not happen until I turned into a middle-aged woman whose baby was starting kindergarten.

One of my clearest memories of cooking for a school assignment was my "brilliant" idea to make *Soupe à L'Oignon* for my middle-school French class. It involved carrying a very heavy, very hot soup pot through the halls and up the stairs of a very large middle school. Memories of the sloshing and spilling of this steaming hot soup still mark one of the stupidest and most terrifying ordeals of my life.

Similar to the hummus recipe, the many years and many times I have prepared onion soup has helped me to perfect it. The recent addition of brandy has definitely taken it to a new level, which would certainly not have occurred to me back in middle school!

FRENCH ONION SOUP

INGREDIENTS

7 cups sliced onions
4 Tbs. unsalted butter
2 Tbs. olive oil
1/4 tsp. honey
3 Tbs. flour
1 quart beef stock
1 quart chicken stock
1/2 cup white wine
1 Tbs. fresh thyme
1 bay leaf
1 Tbs. good-quality brandy
Sea salt and freshly ground
   black pepper
12 slices of baguette (French
   bread)
Olive oil
1 garlic clove, cut in half
1 cup Gruyere cheese, grated

DIRECTIONS

Heat a large soup pot over medium heat and add the onions. After about 5 or so minutes the onions should have given off their liquid and begun to brown. Add the butter, olive oil, and honey and continue to sauté until the onions are soft and golden brown. Add the flour and cook for 5 minutes. Add the stock, wine, thyme, and bay leaf and cook over low heat, partially covered, for about 45 minutes. Add the brandy and simmer for a few minutes. Taste for seasoning, adding salt and pepper, if necessary.

Preheat the oven to 325°. While the soup is cooking, brush the slices of baguette with the olive oil and rub with garlic. Place them on a cookie sheet and bake until golden, turning them over after about 10 minutes. Raise the oven to 375°. Ladle the soup into individual oven-proof soup bowls. Add two slices of toast on top and cover with grated cheese. Bake until the cheese melts, about 10 minutes, and then broil for a minute or two or until the cheese browns. Alternatively, place the toast in bowls, then the soup, and grate the cheese over the soup (without broiling). Serve at once.

YIELD: 6 SERVINGS

My grandmother, Nana, was not a very creative cook but she had a very keen instinct for making food that would appeal to children. One of my favorite dishes that she invented is Fried Spaghetti. I would have it for an after-school snack, for lunch or even for breakfast. It is one of those treats that I still lust after, and my kids enjoy it just as much as I do.

One of the things that make this dish so very special is that you cannot just whip it up at a moment's notice. No, indeed—you must wait! It cannot be made with freshly cooked spaghetti; that is the trick! You must use leftover refrigerated spaghetti that had been previously coated with Del Monte's (*yes, it has to be Del Monte's*) canned tomato sauce! The tomato sauce must have that congealed, almost dried-out, very unappealing appearance so that the spaghetti will crisp up as it cooks. It takes this humble leftover to previously unreachable heights—salty, crunchy, decadent deliciousness! Trust me on this—it is the midnight snack of snacks!

FRIED SPAGHETTI

DIRECTIONS

Take leftover spaghetti that has been previously coated with Del Monte's tomato sauce (yes, it has to be Del Monte's) and salt from the refrigerator and put it in a pan that has a good amount of butter sizzling in it. Over medium heat, cook without stirring until the bottom of the spaghetti is browned.

Carefully turn over in a pancake form with a large spatula and brown thoroughly on the second side. The whole process may take up to half an hour. Enjoy hot—*and by yourself, so no one can see that you've eaten the whole platter!*

My fondest memories of time spent with my mother are at the kitchen table baking cookies together. I suppose that may be the reason I named my cooking school, At the Kitchen Table. Our kitchen table was an old oak table with claws at the base of the legs, which our dog, Ginger, gnawed on at some point. We had a counter that was used on occasion for preparation, but most of the real work of the kitchen was done at this table.

One of the very best cookies we made together was my mother's version of *rugelach*, which are absolutely the very best ever! Rugelach can be translated as *little twists* or *little horns* because the triangles of dough are rolled up into petite shapes. This dough is unusual in that it is simply cream cheese, butter, and flour without any addition of sugar. The dough is then rolled in confectioner's sugar so that the sweetness hits your tongue first without overpowering the flavor of the pastry. My mother always rolled the dough around a filling of strawberry jam, walnuts, raisins, and cinnamon, but there is plenty of room for creativity. These are best eaten the day they are baked, which is not usually a problem at our house.

RUGELACH

INGREDIENTS

Dough
1/2 lb. unsalted butter, softened
8 oz. cream cheese, softened
2 cups all-purpose flour
Confectioner's sugar (for rolling dough)

Filling
1 cup walnuts, broken into medium pieces
1/2 cup raisins
1/2 cup strawberry, raspberry, or apricot jam
1 Tbs. cinnamon

DIRECTIONS

In a medium mixing bowl, combine the butter and cream cheese, and mix until blended. Slowly add the flour until it is all combined. Form into four balls, cover with plastic wrap, and refrigerate for at least 1 hour. Preheat oven to 350°. Combine all the filling ingredients in a medium bowl. Sprinkle the working surface with the confectioner's sugar. Roll out one of the balls, turning dough over as you roll to prevent sticking. Roll into a 1/16-inch-thick circle. Using a sharp knife, cut the dough into 16 pie-shaped pieces. Place 1 tsp. of filling at the wide end of each triangle. Roll up each piece and place with the point underneath on an ungreased cookie sheet. Bake for 20 minutes or until lightly golden.

YIELD: APPROXIMATELY 5 DOZEN

My parents had a very large social circle that shifted over the years, as is often the case. When we lived in Wantagh, their friends were artists, musicians, beatniks—even hippies. As their station in the world evolved, so did their friendships. By the time we moved to Woodbury, my parents' friends were doctors and their wives, and other successful couples. I much preferred the more creative and therefore more interesting friends of the earlier days. Along with the type of friend, the type of party they threw changed significantly. In the old days, popcorn topped with garlic powder was a big hit, but as their income grew, they served more and more elaborate foods. I remember a whole pig on a spit in the backyard!

However, there were many smaller dinner parties as well. At one of these dinner parties, my mother served an apricot brandy sour cream cake that remains in my mind as the most delectable cake I have ever eaten! The sour cream gave the pound cake a moist and tender crumb, and the apricot brandy scented each bite with a perfumed aroma and tangy taste. She succeeded only once in making this perfect cake; every time she made it after that the center of the Bundt was undercooked and heavy. After a couple of tries, she gave up making this wonderful treat! Here is my attempt at recreating this delectable dessert!

APRICOT BRANDY SOUR CREAM CAKE

INGREDIENTS

Batter

2 sticks unsalted butter, room temperature
2 cups white sugar
2 cups all-purpose flour, sifted
1 Tbs. baking powder
1 Tbs. apricot brandy
1 tsp. vanilla extract
5 eggs, room temperature
Apricot jam, 8 oz. jar

DIRECTIONS

Preheat the oven to 350°. Butter and flour a 10-inch Bundt pan. In a standing mixer, cream the butter and sugar until light and fluffy. Add the flour and baking powder and mix in thoroughly. Add the brandy and vanilla and mix again. Add the eggs one at a time, mixing well between additions. Pour into the pan and bake for an hour and a quarter, or until the center is dry when poked with a cake tester. Cool in pan for 10 minutes and turn out onto a rack to cool thoroughly. While cake is cooling, heat the apricot jam in a small pot over moderate heat. Poke holes all over the cake with a toothpick and then brush the cake with the warm jam.

YIELD: 12 SERVINGS

Although the apricot brandy cake was hit or miss, there were definitely other recipes that my mother had perfected over time and were wonderful treats every time she made them. Well, almost every time! Her pecan pie was legendary—sweet, sticky, buttery, nutty—everything you want in a pecan pie and beautiful to behold! The pecans were placed in a perfect intricate design on the top; the thick, yet syrupy, center was sweet but complex; and the crust was crumbly and delicate. The secret to her crust was the combination of sweet butter and lard. My mother often made the pie and then put it in the freezer to have on hand for unexpected company. One day, my dad called in the late afternoon to say he had invited a fellow physician and his wife over for dinner. Yes, I said "invited" not "asked" and so my mother was in a panic over what to serve at such late notice.

I do not recall what my mother threw together for dinner, but I will never forget the pecan pie that she pulled from the freezer to serve for dessert. She proudly placed the pie on the table, cut it into 8 perfect pieces, and served the slices to our guests. The invited guests were from Iran, and they dug into the American treat with great delight. After a few bites, Mrs. Rouhani asked my mother what made the crust so delicate. When she opened her mouth to list the ingredients, she remembered that the Rouhanis were devout Moslems who were forbidden to eat pork products. She decided to fib and leave out the key ingredient: lard!

MOM'S CHOCOLATE PECAN PIE

INGREDIENTS

3 large eggs, beaten
1/2 cup dark brown sugar, packed down
3/4 cup white sugar
3/4 cup dark corn syrup
1/4 cup maple syrup
1 tsp. vanilla extract
3 Tbs. unsalted butter
2 Tbs. bourbon whiskey
1 cup semisweet chocolate chips 3/4–1 cup pecan halves 1 package refrigerated pie crust 1 deep-dish pie pan (9 inch) Vanilla ice cream, optional

DIRECTIONS

Preheat oven to 350°. Allow the pie crust to come to room temperature. Melt the butter, bourbon, and 1/2 cup of the chocolate chips together in a glass bowl in the microwave. Cook at half power, stirring every 30 seconds until just melted. Allow to cool.

In a large bowl, mix the eggs, sugars, syrups, and vanilla. Add the cooled chocolate mixture. Press the piecrust into the pan, leaving extra dough around the edges. Using the tines of a fork, make marks all around the edge. Sprinkle the remaining chocolate chips and 3/4 cup of the pecans on the bottom of the crust. Pour in the mixture. When the pecans float to the top, turn them so that they are all rounded side up and add the rest of them as needed so that the entire surface is covered with pecans. Place the pie pan on top of a cookie sheet (to catch any drips) and bake for about 50 minutes, or until a toothpick emerges clean when poked into the filling about halfway toward the center. Serve with vanilla ice cream, if desired.

SERVES 6–8

My parents were very dedicated atheists but devout Zionists. They had deeply strong feelings for Israel (even buying an apartment in Tel Aviv in 1986), but they never associated with organized religion. They never joined a synagogue, were extremely unkosher (they ate pork and seafood in every way, shape, and form) and even considered belief in God to be naïve. However, we did have a Bible, not the *Old Testament*—but *their* version of the Bible.

It was the *Time/Life Foods of the World* series. They were wonderful hardcover books on international cuisine with stunning photographs, combined with small wire-bound recipe books. They are still the first cookbooks I turn to when I am researching a recipe. As a teenager, I spent many hours reading, browsing, and salivating as I combed through these books. As an adult, I searched resale bookstores for them for years and then found that eBay made it very easy to find them—although I do still prefer browsing the shelves of real bookstores.

When I was fourteen or so, I had a friend whose name was Pam over to the house. We had nothing to do, and I found her quite boring but couldn't send her home, so I suggested that we cook dinner for my family. I suppose that I was pretty persuasive, and she was a bit of a *nebbish* (Yiddish for "a nothing"), and so she agreed. I chose the Scandinavia cookbook in the series and we made something I had never heard of, let alone tasted, before. We made *Frikadeller*, which are Danish meat patties, caramelized potatoes, and cucumber salad. I know that *meat patty* is not a very sexy-sounding dish, but they were the most delicious *hamburgers* I had ever eaten. I just love how juicy, tender, and oniony they are. The secret is the seltzer in the mix, which makes them light and fluffy. Serve them with boiled potatoes and red cabbage!

FRIKADELLER

INGREDIENTS

1/2 lb. ground veal
1/2 lb. ground pork
1 medium onion, grated
3 Tbs. all-purpose flour
1 1/2 cups seltzer
1 egg, beaten
Sea salt and freshly ground
 black pepper, to taste
4 Tbs. unsalted butter
2 Tbs. vegetable oil

DIRECTIONS

In a standing mixer combine the meats, onion, and flour on medium speed. Gradually add the seltzer a few tablespoons at a time until the mixture is light and fluffy. Beat in the egg, salt, and pepper. Cover the bowl and refrigerate for 1 hour. Shape into 8–10 oblong patties. Heat the butter and oil over moderately high heat in a large skillet. Cook the patties about 8 minutes on both sides until deeply browned or until they are cooked through. The juices should run clear when poked with the tip of a sharp knife. Serve at once.

YIELD: 4–6 PATTIES

By the time I got to high school, I had become passionate about cooking and eating. I loved to dance, to act, to paint, to write poetry—but what I loved most was to cook. Thinking about my childhood from a psychological perspective, I believe that cooking fed my soul in a way that my family did not. My mother spent a good deal of my childhood suffering from mental illness, and because of this my father was seldom home. When my mother was in one of her dark times and my dad was away at "work," my brother was most often in the basement making films. He and I had nothing in common and barely spoke to each other, at least not in a civil manner. I did not have a car and was seldom permitted to use the family car.

The school bus brought me home to an empty, fancy house with a Spanish-speaking housekeeper. This did help me learn to speak Spanish, at least kitchen Spanish, but I was alone most afternoons. I don't think I was sad about it because I didn't know there was an alternative.

However, I really enjoyed school and I had more than a few good teachers at Syosset High School. My sociology teacher was one of my favorites, mostly because she enjoyed talking about cooking with me after class. She was a sweet, slightly round African American, whose warmth and Southern manner were exactly what I needed in my early high school years. Her name was Mrs. Ward and I think of her often and have made her recipe for Apple Dumplings repeatedly since she told me how to make them. If you are in a rush, as I have often been when making this, feel free to substitute Bisquick for the batter.

Me, 1970

APPLE DUMPLINGS

INGREDIENTS

3 lbs. peeled, sliced apples (any variety)

1 Tbs. each of cinnamon, sugar, lemon juice, and butter

1 cup all-purpose flour

2 tsp. baking powder

2 Tbs. white sugar

Pinch of sea salt

1/6 cup solid vegetable shortening

1/3 cup whole milk

DIRECTIONS

Place the apples, cinnamon, sugar, lemon juice, and butter in a large pot and sauté over moderate heat until the apples have softened and released some of their juices. While the apples are cooking, add the rest of the ingredients into a medium bowl. Mix until a dough forms. Using a tablespoon, drop the dough into the apple mixture. Cover tightly and cook over low heat for 20 minutes, or until the dough has risen and cooked through. Enjoy while warm!

SERVES 4–6

During my high-school years, my parents' favorite restaurant was Beau Sejour, which served very classic French cuisine in what was once a very large home. The owners were friendly and welcoming and made certain that everyone had a wonderful evening. It was there that I was first exposed to fine French food, and I have many sweet memories of the few times my parents brought my brother and me with them. The waiters were dressed in black and white and brought all the customers their main courses under silver domes, which they removed with a grand flourish for dramatic effect.

My favorite dinner was sorrel soup and chicken with morels, ending with a dessert of chocolate soufflé with vanilla sauce. The soup was refreshingly tart and luxuriously creamy at the same time. The chicken was merely the vehicle for the morel mushrooms, which I savored very slowly, eating a bite of mushroom for every three or four bites of chicken. But the pièce de résistance was the most delicious soufflé. We were required to order it when we ordered our dinners and then needed to wait an extra twenty minutes for it to arrive. When it finally did arrive, it was with yet another grand flourish that the waiter poked the center of the tall soufflé and poured in an entire pitcher of fabulous vanilla sauce. It was swooningly delicious. I never varied my order, and I was never disappointed.

SORREL SOUP

INGREDIENTS

1 lb. fresh sorrel, chiffonade
(sliced into thin ribbons)
6 Tbs. unsalted butter
1 qt. good-quality chicken stock
6 egg yolks
1 cup heavy cream
1 tsp. fresh chervil
Sea salt and freshly ground
black pepper, to taste

DIRECTIONS

Melt 2 Tbs. of the butter in a large skillet and add the sorrel until it has wilted, then remove from the heat. In a large saucepan, heat the stock to barely a simmer. In a small bowl, whisk the egg yolks and the cream, and then gently whisk this mixture into the stock in a steady, thin stream. Reduce the heat and simmer to thicken (but do not allow to boil), then stir in the sorrel. Swirl in the remaining 4 Tbs. of butter and sprinkle with the chervil. Taste for seasoning.

SERVES 4

CHICKEN WITH MORELS

INGREDIENTS

8 chicken thighs, boneless and skinned

2 Tbs. butter

2 Tbs. olive oil

1 cup shallots, peeled and left whole (or halved if they are very large)

1 cup canned or frozen artichoke hearts, defrosted

1 oz. dried morels soaked in warm water or 4–5 fresh morels, sliced thickly

1 cup white wine

1/2 cup chicken stock

2 bay leaves

1 tsp. fresh, or 1/2 tsp dried, thyme

Salt and pepper

1 Tbs. lemon juice

DIRECTIONS

In a large sauté pan, melt 1 Tbs. of the butter with the olive oil. When the butter begins to sizzle, add the chicken a few pieces at a time and brown on both sides, then set aside on a plate. Add the remaining butter to the pan and add the shallots, artichokes, and morels. Add the seasonings and sauté for about ten minutes. Return the chicken to the pan, cover, and cook for about 10 minutes, or until golden. Remove the chicken and vegetables to a serving platter, discarding the bay leaves. Add the wine to the pan and deglaze it by cooking and stirring the browned bits off the bottom of the pan over medium-high heat. Add the chicken broth and reduce by half and then add the lemon juice. Pour the sauce over the chicken and serve.

SERVES 4–6

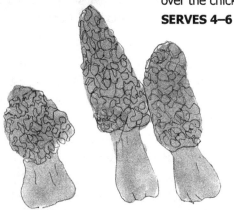

CHOCOLATE SOUFFLÉ

INGREDIENTS

4 oz. bittersweet chocolate, broken into small pieces

1 Tbs. unsalted butter

1/4 cup white sugar

1/4 cup white flour

Pinch of salt

1 cup whole milk

3 eggs and 2 egg whites, at room temperature

Pinch of cream of tartar

1 tsp. vanilla extract

Butter and sugar for soufflé dish

Confectioner's sugar and whipped cream, optional

DIRECTIONS

Preheat oven to 400°. Butter a 1 1/2-quart soufflé dish (you may use a 1-quart soufflé dish and extend the height by buttering a piece of parchment paper and wrapping it around the dish, securing it with kitchen twine), and then sprinkle thoroughly with sugar. Melt the chocolate, butter, and 2 Tbs. of hot water in a small pan or in the microwave at half-power until the chocolate has melted—and stir until the mixture is smooth. Warm the milk in a small pot. Carefully separate the eggs and place the yolks into the bowl of a standing mixer or a medium bowl if you are using a hand-held mixer. Whip the egg yolks along with 1/4 cup of the sugar for a few minutes or until it is pale yellow and fluffy. Add the flour and mix until well-combined and then slowly add half of the milk.

In a medium saucepan, pour in the remaining milk and then add the egg mixture. Bring to a simmer over medium heat, stirring constantly for about 2 minutes. Turn off the heat and whisk in the melted chocolate and the vanilla, and then cover the mixture. Put the egg whites into the cleaned mixing bowl and begin whipping until it starts to foam. Add the cream of tartar and turn up the speed, gradually adding the rest of the sugar until stiff peaks are formed. Put about 1/3 of the egg whites into the chocolate mixture, folding it in until it is well combined. Now fold the chocolate mixture into the egg whites until almost no whites are seen. Spoon into the prepared dish. Bake for 15 minutes and then turn the oven down to 375° and bake until it has puffed and become golden. If you made a paper collar, remove it now, and then dust with the confectioner's sugar and serve immediately with whipped cream, if desired. **SERVES 4–6**

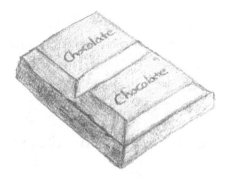

I have always enjoyed identifying wild mushrooms and—when I am certain of their safety—cooking them. When I was about twelve years old, I spotted some puffball mushrooms in our backyard. I now know that they are pretty much foolproof, as there are no toxic varieties. At the time, as a budding would-be mycologist (mushroom scientist) it was pretty foolhardy of me to believe they were safe to eat. However, I have a daredevil streak in me, so I cooked them for the family. My father tentatively tasted them and then declared that he was not interested in playing mushroom roulette in the future; end of story!

When my husband and I bought our three-acre plot of land and its 1860s one-room schoolhouse for our second home in Columbia County, New York, I was delighted to find a myriad of wild mushrooms in the fields. My children and I have spent many happy hours identifying and sometimes cooking them. One day, a number of years ago, I prepared a variety that I had never tasted before, *Stropharia*, after doing extensive research on them. My mushroom book suggested that when trying a new mushroom, it is wise to have one adult who can drive refrain from tasting it so that he or she can drive the rest of the diners to the emergency room, if necessary.

While we were eating those *Stropharia* mushrooms, my daughter, then about fourteen years old, noticed that my husband was not eating them. I explained that the book had cautioned about having a driver available, and she declared, "Why are you letting me eat them? I am only a child!" We had a good laugh, but she was right, you have to be extremely cautious when eating wild mushrooms. I have taken mold spores, enlisted the help of a local expert, and limited our enjoyment to the few unmistakable varieties.

This recipe uses either wild—or plain, old, cultivated—white mushrooms, but it is a delightful treat, nonetheless.

MUSHROOMS AL AJILLO

INGREDIENTS

3 Tbs. extra-virgin olive oil
1 lb. mushrooms (wild or domestic), sliced
2 cloves garlic, sliced
1 Tbs. fresh parsley, minced
1/4 tsp. hot pepper flakes, or to taste
Salt and freshly ground black pepper, to taste

DIRECTIONS

Preheat a large cast-iron skillet over moderately high heat. When hot, add the oil and allow to heat for a minute. Add the mushrooms, stir for a minute, and add the garlic. Cook until the mushrooms have become wilted and add the hot pepper, salt, and pepper. Taste for seasoning, turn off the heat, and add the parsley. Serve at once.

SERVES FOUR (AS AN APPETIZER)

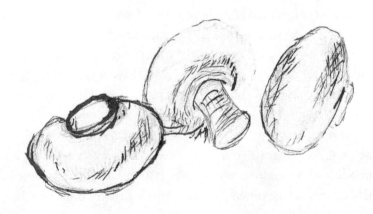

Almost every day of my life in Woodbury, I felt Jewish in one way or another. It doesn't mean we were in any way a religious family; as I have written, my father ridiculed the whole idea of faith. My parents even belonged to a group that called themselves the Yom Kippur Club. This group of friends did not work on the holiest day of the Jewish calendar, but they were certainly not going to a synagogue to pray or even to fast on this, the only, fast day of the year. No, they would choose a different restaurant each Yom Kippur to have lunch together. Blasphemy, I know, but this is how they thumbed their noses at their tradition. I suppose every generation has to rebel, somehow.

However, we did follow many Jewish family rituals, such as lighting the Sabbath candles, celebrating Hanukkah and Passover. It is traditional for a Jewish family to light the Sabbath candles and say a blessing over them, over the sweet Manischewitz wine and over *challah* bread. My mother was a really great baker, and her challah was unmatched by any bakery in the area. She certainly did not bake challah every Friday, but when she did, there was never a crumb left for French toast on Sunday.

LORA'S CHALLAH

INGREDIENTS

1 Tbs. dry yeast

1 cup warm water

1 Tbs. white sugar

5 cups all-purpose flour

1/2 Tbs. salt

1/3 cup honey

2 extra-large eggs

1/4 cup vegetable oil

Egg for glazing

Raisins and/or sesame or poppy
seeds

DIRECTIONS

Proof the yeast by mixing 1 cup of the warm water with the yeast and sugar in a glass measuring cup. Mix well with a wooden spoon until the yeast has dissolved. Put aside for 5 minutes to make sure that a foamy head has started to form on the top. (If it does not foam, you will need to use a different package of yeast.) In a very large mixing bowl, pour in the flour and salt to form a mountain. Make a well in the center and pour in the yeast mixture. Using a wooden spoon, begin to mix the flour into the center. Add the honey, stir in more of the flour. Add the eggs one at a time, mixing in the flour as you go. Now mix in all the flour and the oil. The dough should not be sticky; if not, add a little more flour. Divide the dough into four equal parts. Using the metal blade of a food processor, put the dough into the machine and let it run until a ball is formed. Repeat with the other pieces of dough. Alternatively, knead the dough on a floured surface for 10 minutes, or until the dough is soft and pliable.

Heat oven to 140° and then turn the oven off. Place the four balls of dough in a large greased mixing bowl and cover with plastic wrap. Place in the oven and allow to rise until double in bulk in about an hour. Divide each ball into four equal parts. Roll the pieces into balls and then into long ropes. Take four ropes and press the four ends together. Braid the four pieces together by starting with an outside rope and going over and under until you reach the end. Pull the pieces tightly as you go to form a higher loaf. Repeat with the remaining loaves. You can also divide the four pieces of dough into sixteen pieces each and form challah knots by making long ropes and tying them into knots. Place each challah onto a greased cookie sheet and cover with plastic. Allow to rise for about 1 hour. Preheat the oven to 375°.

Mix the egg with 1 Tbs. of water and brush the glaze all over the challahs. Sprinkle with the seeds. Bake for about 30 minutes or until golden. If making rolls, they need to bake for only about 15 minutes. They freeze well.

YIELD: 2 LOAVES. (RECIPE CAN BE DOUBLED.)

Every Christmas vacation and often in the summer we piled in to my father's Lincoln Continental and drove almost nonstop from Long Island to Miami Beach. My father would wake us at four in the morning to start the excruciatingly long drive to our first night in Savannah, Georgia. My brother, Owen, and I barely ever communicated when we were at home, so all those many hours side-by-side without so much as a radio—never mind a cell phone—was pure torture. The only diversion we had was that we used to make up songs to sing; I still remember many of them. Owen became a lyricist, and I would venture to say that this is where it all began. As I think back on it now, it seems very sweet and creative and helped make the time pass as pleasantly as possible.

Staying with my father's mother, Bubbe, was always an adventure. She was a rather careless housekeeper but loved gardening and cooking and showing us off to her friends at her beach club, where she played canasta and mahjong. My parents did not stay at her small home but instead stayed at the nearby Howard Johnson hotel, which had a pool. We swam at the pool and went to the beach, visited with our cousins, and I learned about gardening and Jewish cooking, which are still two of the things I enjoy most.

But what we looked forward to most when we came to Miami was going to Shorty's Barbeque in Homestead, about an hour south of my grandmother's home. The meat was incredible—smokey, tender, flavorful, and served with a fantastic vinegar-based sauce that contained the drippings from the meat. My grandmother was kosher, so she only ate their chicken (which was assuredly not kosher and which I am sure was more delicious because the chicken was basted with those porky drippings). However, it was the ribs and pork sandwiches that we came there to eat.

We would bring the leftovers back to Bubbe's, but she insisted that they be very well covered in aluminum and plastic in order to allow the *treife* (unkosher) pork in her refrigerator. I have never had barbeque that has come even close to the pig heaven that Shorty's sent us to. This is a recipe that my father hand-wrote and gave to me.

CHOPPED PORK BARBECUE

INGREDIENTS

1 pork loin roast, 4–5 pounds
1 medium onion, chopped
1 cup cider vinegar
3/4 cup ketchup
1/2 cup Worcestershire sauce
3 Tbs. dry Colman's mustard
1/4 cup honey or brown sugar
1 tsp. kosher salt
1 tsp. Tabasco sauce
2 garlic cloves, minced

DIRECTIONS

Combine all the sauce ingredients and pour over the pork loin in a sealed plastic bag. Refrigerate for 3 hours. Preheat the oven to 325°. Place the pork loin and sauce into a roasting pan and cook for 2 1/2 hours. Remove from oven and allow to cool for 20 minutes. Pull the pork into shreds and serve on Kaiser rolls with coleslaw.

SERVES 8–10

When I was a senior in high school, I took an elective class called International Foods. It was in the Home Economics department and was taught by the Head Cheerleading coach. I admit that I was embarrassed to be taking a Home Ec. class, and my group of friends definitely did not include anyone on the cheerleading team—the debate team, maybe. I LOVED the cooking class, but at the time it was almost unheard of for a woman to be a chef, so I put aside my passion and only cooked for friends and family.

About thirty years later, when I had started teaching cooking, I offered a catered dinner at a fundraiser for my kids' school, and it was purchased by a lovely family who wanted me to be their private chef. I was very flattered but lived hours away from them, which made it impossible. The dish that won them over was a recipe that I learned in that high-school cooking class. It is a Russian recipe that seems very simple, with only a few ingredients put together in a very straightforward style, but the combination of apples, butter, apricot jam, rum, cinnamon, and high-quality white bread make for an outstanding dessert that can be prepared for any dinner party.

APPLE CHARLOTTE

INGREDIENTS

1 loaf thinly sliced Arnold's white sandwich bread

5 lbs. cooking apples, peeled and sliced thinly

5 Tbs. water

3/4 cup white sugar

1 tsp. ground cinnamon

1 cup unsalted butter

3/4 cup apricot preserves

1 Tbs. vanilla extract

1/3 cup dark rum

DIRECTIONS

In a large saucepan, combine the apples, water, and sugar—and bring to a boil over high heat. Reduce the heat to low and cover the pan. Cook for about 30 minutes or until the apples are tender. Uncover and cook over medium heat, stirring frequently, for about 15 minutes or until it has become a thick puree. Add the cinnamon and refrigerate.

Preheat the oven to 375°. Butter the insides of a 1 1/2-quart casserole dish. Cut the crusts off the bread and cut half the bread in half to make triangles, and the other half in four to make squares. Melt half of the butter in a large sauté pan and add half of the squares, turning the pieces over when they are golden. Dip the remaining bread into the rest of the melted butter. Place half of the triangles in the bottom of the casserole dish, reserving the other triangles for the top. Arrange the squares along the sides of the dish. Pour the apple mixture into the dish. Place the last of the triangles on top of the apples. Cover any exposed areas with more bread that has been dipped in butter. Bake for one hour or until golden brown. Allow to cool for 30 minutes and then invert onto a dish. While the charlotte is cooling, combine the preserves, vanilla, and rum in a small saucepan and heat over a moderate flame, stirring until the preserves have melted. Pour the sauce over the top of the charlotte.

SERVES 8

My friends were on the debate team or the mathletes—not that I fit into either of those groups very well. We all belonged to the Forensic League, which was dramatic reading and writing at a competitive level. The debate team was part of this league, as well. I competed at a couple of meets, doing dramatic prose readings of the Southern writer, Eudora Welty, and other poets.

By my third meet, which was the qualifying competition for the Nationals, I placed in the top group and was sent to the Catholic League National Competition in New Orleans. I don't know why my New York Public School was included in this competition, but it wasn't to my advantage. I inappropriately chose to read a passage from Eudora Welty, and found that it was not a good idea for a New York Jew to perform the work of a Southern Catholic. I made it to the semifinals but disappointingly, not to the finals. However, it was a great experience for a high school student, and I drowned my sorrows in delicious Creole food.

My father had been a student at Louisiana State University and had spent a good deal of time in New Orleans, so he gave me some suggestions as to what and where to eat when we arrived. My teammates were more than happy to accompany me to Café du Monde for scrumptious beignets and to other spots for bread pudding with whiskey sauce. However, they were a little skeptical about my unending search for crawfish.

We ended up in a small but refined café where the crawfish were served out of the shell in an étouffée, or stew. I was very disappointed, as I had imagined a huge pile of them in their bright red shells ready to be torn apart and devoured. The next year, I returned with my family and feasted on mounds of crawfish in the town of Lafayette, the "crawfish capitol of the world"!

My friends and I had bread pudding almost every day, and I brought back the recipe with me and made it successfully for years to come. It became a favorite of my husband, Peter, when we started dating in college, and we made it together for friends and family for many years.

BREAD PUDDING WITH WHISKEY SAUCE

BREAD PUDDING

INGREDIENTS

Softened butter to grease the baking dish

1 loaf of day-old French bread, ripped into chunks

1 quart whole milk

3 eggs, beaten

1 1/2 cups sugar

2 Tbs. vanilla extract

DIRECTIONS

Preheat oven to 350°. Grease a 13 x 9-inch baking dish with the butter and set aside. Place the bread into a large bowl and cover with the milk. In a small bowl, mix together the eggs, sugar, and vanilla. Pour this over the bread mixture and mix thoroughly. Pour the mixture evenly into the baking dish. Place the dish into a large roasting pan and add hot water into the pan until it reaches halfway up the baking dish. Bake for about an hour, or until it has set.

WHISKEY SAUCE

INGREDIENTS

1 stick unsalted butter, sliced into bits

1 cup sugar

1 egg yolk

4 oz. bourbon whiskey

DIRECTIONS

Melt the butter over low heat in a small saucepan. Add the sugar and stir until the sugar has melted. Add the egg yolk and stir until the mixture has thickened, but do not allow to simmer. Remove from the heat and cool to room temperature. Add the bourbon and serve at once.

SERVES 6–8

There were more than four hundred seniors graduating with me at Syosset High School in June 1974, and because of rain, the ceremony had to be held in the gym. Therefore, only two guests were permitted for each student. Bubbe had flown in from Miami to attend, so my father did not see me graduate. For all these years, I was very hurt thinking that he didn't care about watching me graduate. I think I now understand that it was breaking his heart that his little girl was moving away from home. I, on the other hand, was all too eager to leave Woodbury and start a new life on my own.

Syosset H.S., June 1974 (Dad made the pendant.)

CHAPTER 3

CONNECTICUT COLLEGE
1974-1978

I arrived at Connecticut College in early September 1974 with my father and two suitcases. I cannot believe how little I brought with me, but I had no help packing and threw together just the barest of necessities. My mother had begun a downward spiral into depression brought on by my leaving for college, and that is why she did not join us. I remember my dad taking me to the bank and teaching me how to write a check and boasting that he was giving me $1,000 in spending money for the year. That seemed like a lot of money at the time, but now I recall that it was just barely enough to get me through early Spring, and I was terrified to ask for more.

My room was on the top floor, four flights up, at the Harkness dormitory, which was the designated "quiet dorm." I had chosen to be in this dorm because I knew that I was not the party-going type and needed peace and quiet in order to study. My roommate, Sarah, from Nutley, New Jersey, was not at all the roommate I expected. She and I just never had much to talk about, and we didn't click. I suppose that whoever decided to put us together must have thought we would get along. It made sense that she and I would have a lot in common, as she, too, was from a wealthy Jewish suburban family, but that was where the similarities ended, and we never connected. It was a very long year of trying to avoid each other.

Other than the roommate situation, I was very happy at

Connecticut College. It was a beautiful campus and offered interesting classes, a varied student body, and professors who cared about the students. At my first lecture in Anthropology 101, I was sitting in the front row of a large lecture hall right next to a young man I had seen in my dorm. At one point, our arms touched, and I truly felt electricity go up and down my arm when they did. After all these many years, I thought that it was by chance that we were sitting next to one another. However, I just found out that this young man, Peter, who is my husband of forty-one years, sat down next to me on purpose—so sweet!

Now you know where this story is going! A few days after this electrifying introduction my roommate, Sarah, asked me if I would like to go on a double date with her and her boyfriend and his friend to celebrate Rosh Hashanah, the Jewish New Year. I was dating someone from high school, but I thought I would do Sarah a favor and go, because the two of them didn't have a car, and this friend of theirs did. We went to dinner in Mystic at The Seaman's Inn, and by the time we got to dessert, I found myself feeding Peter strawberries from my Strawberries Romanov. (Thank you, Sarah!)

STRAWBERRIES ROMANOV

INGREDIENTS

1 pint best-quality vanilla ice cream, melted

1 pint sour cream

2 ounces orange liqueur

2 tsp. pure vanilla extract

2 cups heavy cream, whipped

4 pints fresh strawberries, hulled and sliced

fresh mint for garnish

DIRECTIONS

In a medium bowl, blend the ice cream, sour cream, liqueur, and vanilla with a rubber spatula. Fold in the whipped cream. Divide the strawberries among 8 serving dishes and then top with the cream mixture. Garnish with the mint and serve at once.

SERVES 8

When we returned to our dorm, I was just a little surprised when Peter kissed me good night, because it was on my mind that I was technically still dating my high-school boyfriend, Jeff. I could not deny the heart fluttering that was going on, but when I returned to my room, Sarah asked how the date went and I replied, "Well, he's nice but he's not Jeff!"

At the same time, Peter returned to his room and wrote his high school girlfriend, Edith, a "Dear Jane" letter telling her that he had met someone else. It is still hard for me to believe how quickly he knew that we would work out. I, on the other hand, needed some time and didn't tell Jeff anything. When I went home for Thanksgiving and saw Jeff, he knew from my hesitant kiss "hello" that something was up and immediately asked me what was going on. That was the last time we went on a date. Many, many years later, perhaps more than thirty years, I went with two of my kids to see Jeff perform on the drums in Great Barrington, Massachusetts, the town next to ours. It was definitely an awkward situation but very reassuring to find that Jeff was just as sweet as I remembered him to be.

Not long after the strawberry evening, Peter and I went to Manhattan on our first official big date to see Barry Manilow in concert. Yes, I am aware of how corny that sounds, but at the time Barry was a very big deal; his song "Mandy" was at the top of the charts. Before the concert, we went to an Italian restaurant whose name has completely gone out of my head.

I think that I must have been showing off my culinary sophistication by ordering the *osso buco*. I truly loved it mostly for the scrumptious marrow in the veal bones, which I scooped out with the marrow spoon that the restaurant provided. The look of disgust on Peter's face was hysterical but did not dissuade me from scraping out every morsel! He managed to overlook this indiscretion in my taste then, and I still order osso buco whenever it is on the menu, and Peter has almost adjusted to this obsession.

OSSO BUCCO

INGREDIENTS

8 pieces of 2-inch thick sliced
 veal shank

1 large onion, chopped

2 carrots, chopped

2 celery stalks, chopped

2 Tbs. unsalted butter

2 garlic cloves, minced

2-inch piece of lemon peel

4 Tbs. extra-virgin olive oil

1/2 cup white flour

1 cup white wine

2 cups beef broth

1 large can chopped tomatoes
 1 tsp. fresh (or 1/2 tsp.
 dried) thyme, oregano, and
 basil, chopped

2 bay leaves

1/4 cup fresh parsley (save for
 garnish)

Salt and pepper, to taste

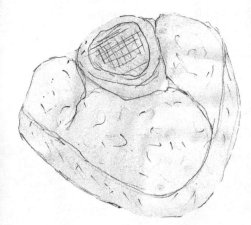

DIRECTIONS

Preheat the oven to 350°. Find a large, heavy casserole with a lid that will fit all the meat in a single layer (or use two smaller vessels). Place the butter in the casserole and heat over a medium flame until the butter sizzles. Add the onions, carrots, and celery and cook for about 5 minutes or until soft. Add the lemon peel and the garlic. Remove to a bowl. Add the olive oil to the pan. Put the flour, salt, and pepper onto a plate and dredge the veal in it, shaking off any extra flour. Brown the meat in the pan on all sides and remove to a plate. Add the wine while scraping up all the browned bits on the bottom of the pan. Return the meat to the pan and cover with the vegetables. Add the tomatoes, herbs (except the parsley), and the salt and pepper. Add enough beef broth so that the liquid fills the casserole at least halfway, making sure that the meat is covered by at least 2 inches. Cover the casserole and cook for two hours, basting the meat every half hour. Remove the meat to a serving platter and cook the sauce over high heat until it thickens. Add the parsley and taste for seasoning. Serve with pasta or risotto.

SERVES 8

At that same restaurant, we had a life-changing dessert; as much as dessert can change your life, this one certainly did. Not knowing what was to come, we ordered *zabaglione*, which was prepared tableside for two. I think that there is nothing more romantic than food prepared tableside for two. Why don't more restaurants offer this kind of service anymore? Well, maybe there are places that do, but we now live in the Berkshires, which is known for its informality. You can literally wear anything, anytime, anywhere—which is why we like it, so why am I complaining?

But I digress, the waiter came to the table and cracked open several eggs and began to whisk the yolks in a copper pot over a small flame until they became lemon-colored and fluffy. He then added sugar, and finally, Marsala wine. When he had achieved the right texture, he poured the elixir into waiting champagne glasses which contained a few ruby-colored raspberries and presented us with this most luxurious dessert.

We made this dessert over and over again until we could replicate it ourselves. We very quickly learned that there are many tricks needed to successfully make a marvelous zabaglione. We threw out many, many egg mixtures that had curdled because the heat was too high or the heat was too low or who knows whatever else we did incorrectly. We did achieve success from time to time—but there never were guarantees—so when we did, it was as though we had created a masterpiece. However, not one of them remain as luscious to me as my memory of that original creation.

ZABAGLIONE

INGREDIENTS

4 egg yolks
1/4 cup white sugar
1/2 cup Marsala wine
1/4 cup fresh raspberries or
strawberries

DIRECTIONS

Place the raspberries or strawberries equally into the bottom of 4 champagne glasses. In a standing mixer, whip the egg yolks with the sugar for a few minutes until they are pale and creamy. While they are whipping, heat water in the bottom of a double boiler until it comes to a simmer. Transfer the egg mixture to the top of the double boiler and add the wine. Continue to beat the mixture until it forms soft mounds. Spoon the zabaglione on top of the raspberries and serve immediately.

SERVES 4

Peter, flag football, 1974

In January of our freshman year, I was told to come down the four flights to the only telephone in the dorm to receive a phone call. It was from Pat, Peter's mom, much to my shock and surprise. She called to say that it would soon be Peter's birthday, and she wanted to make certain that I would take him out to dinner at an appropriately fancy restaurant. She said that it was a necessity that he have caviar and Crêpes Suzette for this birthday. The World Wide Web had not been invented yet, so I needed to call restaurant after restaurant to learn if they had caviar and crêpes, but to no avail. I did finally find a restaurant on the waterfront in Stonington that served crêpes stuffed with crabmeat, so that is where we went.

We each ordered the crêpes which were very delicious but extremely rich. From living in a student dorm, my stomach was unaccustomed to such rich food, so I spent an embarrassingly good deal of time in the bathroom. However, I made it back to the table for dessert, grasshopper pie! The name was so intriguing, and it was something so distant from my upbringing, so very *WASPY*. My mother would never serve a frozen dessert made with peppermint-flavored whipped cream on a chocolate cookie crust. Nevertheless, I believe I ate every morsel of that pie—grasshoppers and all! As I think back on that meal, I do believe it was all that cream that did me in.

GRASSHOPPER PIE

INGREDIENTS

1 package chocolate wafer
   cookies
2 Tbs. unsalted butter, melted
1 half-pint heavy cream
1/4 cup sugar
1 tsp. peppermint extract
1 semisweet chocolate bar

DIRECTIONS

Place the cookies into a sealable plastic bag and, using a rolling pin, crush them finely. Pour into a medium bowl and blend in the melted butter. Press the mixture into a pie plate. Whip the cream, adding the sugar before the cream becomes too thick. Stir in the peppermint extract and taste to see if the cream needs more sugar or extract. Pile the cream into the pie plate and freeze for at least 3 hours. Remove when completely frozen and decorate by shaving the chocolate bar, using a vegetable peeler.

SERVES 6

One of my floor-mates that first year was Donald Rumsfeld's daughter, who was then the Secretary of Defense. I remember that my parents came to visit and my mother brought a tin of homemade *hamantaschen* cookies for the Jewish holiday of Purim. I had no idea who Donald Rumsfeld was, but my parents were so impressed and urged me to offer one of the cookies to his daughter. I did so hesitantly and was met with little enthusiasm and perhaps a touch of disdain, which I took as a sign that she was not interested in my Jewish cookies. That was the one and only time that we ever spoke. My mother's hamantaschen were delicious, as were all of her baked goods, and I thoroughly enjoyed the rest of them.

There was always a big debate in my house over which type of hamantaschen we preferred: yeast or cookie—and over which type of filling: apricot, prune, or poppy. I always preferred the yeast type, which my grandmother Bubbe would send up from Miami, and I have always adored poppy seeds.

A few years ago, we all went to Poland to attend the wedding of our son Zach and his wife, Roza. There, I saw fields and fields of poppies, which had mostly dried onto the pods. I had never seen how poppy seeds grow and thought my cooking students would be interested to see them as well. So I picked a few pods, wrapped them in a tissue and stuck them in the bottom of my suitcase. When we arrived home, I looked for them, but all that was left was the tissue. I suppose they were confiscated, as poppies are the source for opium. Oh, well.

Hamantaschen are pocket-shaped to hold the filling. *Taschen* is "pocket" in Yiddish, and they are called *Oznei Haman* in Hebrew, which translates as "the ears of Haman." Haman was an evil minister in ancient Persia who tried to have all the Jews in Persia annihilated but failed because Queen Esther, who was Jewish, warned the King about the plan. I have heard that it is an ancient tradition to symbolize your enemy in your food and then consume them, and that is one theory for the custom of hamantaschen.

HAMANTASCHEN

INGREDIENTS

Cookie Dough

1 cup Crisco shortening

1 1/2 cups sugar

5 eggs

1/3 cup orange juice

1 tsp. vanilla extract

6 cups all-purpose flour

4 tsp. baking powder

1/8 tsp. salt

DIRECTIONS

Preheat oven to 350°. Cream the shortening and sugar together. Add the eggs one at a time, mixing well after each addition. Add the orange juice and vanilla. Sift together the flour, baking powder, and salt. Add to the egg mixture and mix well. Roll into a ball and place on a lightly floured board. Roll out to 1/4-inch thickness. Use a large glass to cut circles in the dough and fill with 1 tsp. of the desired fillings, pinching 3 corners to make a triangular shape. Bake until lightly browned, about 12 minutes.

Yeast Dough

1 cup milk

1/2 cup sugar

1 1/2 tsp. salt

1/2 cup warm water

2 packages yeast

2 eggs, beaten

3 to 4 Tbs. vegetable oil

6 cups all-purpose flour

2 egg yolks

2 tsp. water

Poppy Seed Filling

1/2 cup poppy seeds

1/4 cup currants

1/4 cup honey

Mix the ingredients to form a
    paste.

Other Fillings: Prune butter
    (Lekvar), apricot jam, Nutella

Preheat oven to 375°. Scald the milk, add the sugar and salt, and cool to room temperature. Pour the warm water into a large, warmed bowl. Sprinkle in the yeast, stir until dissolved. Add the milk mixture, eggs, and oil. Stir in 2 cups of the flour and mix well until blended. Add enough flour to make a soft dough. Turn out onto a floured board. Knead well until smooth and elastic, about 5 minutes. Place dough in a lightly oiled bowl, cover and allow to rise in a warm place until doubled in size, about 1 hour. Punch down and divide in half. Roll out onto a lightly floured board and cut into circles. Fill with 1 tsp of the desired filling. Pinch 3 corners to make a triangle and allow to rise for half an hour, and then brush with the egg yolks mixed with the water. Bake until light brown, about 25 minutes.

About a month after we had started dating, Peter invited me to his parents' home in Larchmont, New York, for the fiftieth-birthday celebration for his father, Ed. It was quite an introduction to the family—as soon as we arrived, we looked all over the house for his mother; we finally found her in the swimming pool, in the buff! I was apoplectic and pretty much ran back into the house. I settled on a couch in the living room, and a few minutes later, his mother yelled, "Get off the couch, Julie!" In complete horror and dismay, I jumped up, only to find that one of their Airedale Terriers shared my name.

Later that evening, I was sitting all alone once again in the living room when I overheard Peter's older sister counsel him about not marrying the first girl he dates in college. I couldn't believe she was talking about me with the door open. I was extremely embarrassed and uncomfortable for the remainder of our visit. I now understand that she was only trying to protect her brother from me, not knowing me at all, but it sure was a sticky moment.

Peter and Rugby in the pool, 1974

Peter's mother's name was Joan, but everyone called her "Pat" because, as the story went, her grandmother used to call her "pet" and that became Pat. She never met her birth father, and her mother remarried several times. At eight years of age, Pat was called as a witness in her parents' very public divorce trial. She was sent to boarding school after that and had an extremely strained relationship with her mother, Louise, from then on.

I met Louise only a few times, and she seemed to be a very cold and bitter woman. She once wildly accused me of stealing her mink coat! Peter had almost no relationship at all with his grandmother, who lived in California. At the age of ninety-five she was moved to Riverdale, to a nursing home close to our house. We saw her occasionally until she died at the age of ninety-nine.

Pat employed a cook, housekeeper, butler, and laundress in her household and had no interest in cooking—or much else, for that matter—but she had definite likes and dislikes in food. I learned very early on, that Pat loved the Italian Christmas sweet bread, *panettone.* In an attempt to gain her affection, I baked one for her. I had never baked a panettone and never even tasted one, but I made an enormous one for her.

Peter, Adam, Pat, and Grandma Lou, 1983

It was a huge, sweet brioche studded with candied fruit that took three risings and many hours to construct and bake, and I was very excited to taste it after I gave it to her. However, in what I soon learned was her typical behavior, she carried the panettone up to her bedroom and ate the entire thing by herself. I have never made another one!

PANETTONE

INGREDIENTS

3 packages dry yeast

1/4 cup sugar

1/3 cup warm water

6 egg yolks

1 tsp. vanilla extract

1/2 tsp. finely grated lemon
peel

1/2 tsp. salt

2–3 cups all-purpose flour

1 stick unsalted butter, room
temperature

1/4 cup dark raisins

1/4 cup golden raisins

1/4 cup dried cherries

2 Tbs. melted butter

DIRECTIONS

Combine the yeast, 1 tsp. of the sugar, and water in a glass measuring cup and stir until all is dissolved. Place in a warm, draft-free place like the turned-off oven and allow to foam for 3–5 minutes. Transfer to a large mixing bowl and add the egg yolks, vanilla, lemon peel, and the rest of the sugar and salt, mixing well. Add the flour 1 cup at a time to form a soft dough. Add the butter one-third at a time, mixing with your hands, adding a little more flour as needed to form a heavy dough and then knead for 10 minutes to form a smooth and shiny dough. Form into a ball, place in an oiled bowl, cover with a lid, and place in the same warm spot for 30 minutes to double in bulk.

Preheat the oven to 400°. Punch the dough down with your fist and gently knead in the dried fruit, being careful not to over-mix. Shape into a ball and place on a parchment-covered baking sheet. Wrap the dough in a 5-inch-wide strip of buttered brown paper and tie with a string. Set to rise again (not in the preheating oven), and after about 15 minutes, brush with the melted butter. Bake for 10 minutes, then reduce the heat to 350° and brush again with the butter. Bake for 30 minutes, brushing with the butter after the first 15 minutes. Remove from the oven when it is golden brown and cool on a rack.

Another ridiculous effort on my part to impress my future mother-in-law was the time I made her an Apple *Tarte Tatin*. Once again, I had never made one before but I had enjoyed them many times, especially at a fabulous restaurant in Manhattan that has since disappeared, Max's Kansas City. This tart was apparently the creation of the Tatin sisters in France and is basically an upside-down cake with tender, deeply caramelized apples, best served warm with crème fraîche.

This time I spent many hours making certain the apples were lined up in a consecutive circular pattern, that the caramel was dark and bubbling, and that the crust was crisp and buttery. I handed this marvelous pièce de résistance to Pat, hoping against hope that she would share even a small sliver of it with the rest of us. However, true to her style, she squirrelled it away to her room and ate it all herself. I have made many Tarte Tatin's since then and have taught it several times. I enjoy it every time and it is an impressive sight (without the waiting time that panettone requires).

APPLE TARTE TATIN

INGREDIENTS

8 firm-textured apples, peeled
and thinly sliced

1/2 cup unbleached sugar

1 tsp. cinnamon

2 Tbs. softened unsalted butter
(for baking dish)

4 Tbs. unsalted butter, melted

1 cup flour

1/4 cup sugar

1 egg and 2 egg yolks

Pinch of salt

Crème fraîche or ice cream,
optional

DIRECTIONS

Preheat the oven to 375 °. Toss the apples with 1/3 of the sugar and the cinnamon in a large bowl. Use the softened butter to heavily coat a 9-inch cast-iron skillet. Sprinkle half of the remaining sugar to coat the dish. Add the apples and pour the melted butter on top. Sprinkle the apples with the remaining sugar. Place over medium heat on the stove. Place the flour and sugar in a medium bowl or the bowl of a food processor and mix thoroughly. Using a mixer or the metal blade of the processor, add butter. Mix until the mixture becomes crumbly. Add the eggs and salt and run until it forms a ball. If it seems dry, add a teaspoon or two of ice water. Lightly flour a board and a rolling pin and roll out the dough into a 1/8-inch circle. Remove the apples from the heat. Roll the circle onto the rolling pin and place onto the apples. Poke several holes in the surface to allow the steam to escape. Bake in the lower third of the oven for 45–60 minutes or until a thick brown syrup has formed on top of the apple mixture. Cover the tart with aluminum foil if it is browning before the apples have cooked. Remove from the oven and invert immediately onto a serving platter. Serve warm with crème fraîche or ice cream.

SERVES 4-6

Without a doubt the most ridiculous example of my great need to please this woman was the time I baked a *sacher torte* and had to transport it from my parents' home on Long Island across the Whitestone Bridge to Westchester County. Sacher tortes originated in Vienna and believe it or not, there has been an almost century-old legal dispute as to whether the pastry chef at the Sacher hotel or the pastry chef at Demel's Pastry Shop was its first creator.

When freshly made, it is my absolute favorite chocolate cake: apricot jam in the center and chocolate *ganache* dripped down the sides! It is a torte because of the lower proportion of flour to the rest of the ingredients, which makes for a dense crumb. It is often very dry, and so it usually requires a lot of *shlag* (freshly-made whipped cream). I ordered it at Demel's a few years ago and to tell the truth, I was a bit disappointed. I haven't made it to Sacher's, but will definitely go the next time we are in Vienna.

I made a gorgeous, huge, shiny sacher torte for Pat and had it on my lap for the long drive from my parents' house to Peter's parents. Peter was driving and I had been afraid to put the cake down anywhere in the car for fear of it sliding around. All was going well until we were halfway across the Whitestone Bridge when Peter had to stop short so as not to hit the car in front of us. My arm went right through the cake; up to the elbow! I very carefully extracted it inch by inch, licked off my chocolate-coated arm, and set about patching it up until it looked halfway decent. What a nightmare! I gave to Pat and I don't think she even noticed the damage as she took off up to her bedroom with it! That was the very last pastry I ever made for her!

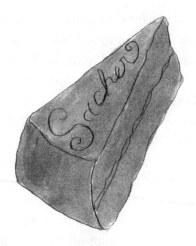

SACHER TORTE

INGREDIENTS

Cake

6 oz. semisweet chocolate chips
1 stick unsalted butter
1 tsp. vanilla extract
8 egg yolks
10 egg whites
Pinch of salt
1/2 cup sugar
1 cup sifted all-purpose flour
3/4 cup apricot or raspberry
    jam

Glaze

3 oz. unsweetened chocolate,
    broken into small pieces
1 cup heavy cream
3/4 cup sugar
1 tsp. corn syrup
1 egg
1 tsp. vanilla extract

DIRECTIONS

Preheat the oven to 350°. Cut 9-inch circles of parchment paper to fit two 9-inch cake pans. Spray the pans with non-stick spray and then place the parchment paper in each pan. Butter the paper and then flour the pans. Melt the chocolate chips and butter together in a double boiler, stirring occasionally until they blend and add the vanilla. Place the egg yolks in a small bowl and whisk until smooth and then stir in the chocolate mixture. In a standing mixer or large bowl, beat the egg whites with the salt until they foam and then add the sugar one tablespoon at a time, mixing on high and continuing to beat until they form stiff peaks. Mix a few tablespoons of the egg whites into the chocolate and then add the chocolate to the egg whites, gently folding with a rubber spatula until they are blended.

Sprinkle in the flour and fold in thoroughly. Pour the batter into the pans and bake in the middle of the oven for 25 minutes or until a toothpick poked in the center emerges clean. Cool for 5 minutes and then turn out onto cake racks to thoroughly cool.

In a small saucepan combine the chocolate chips, cream, sugar, and corn syrup. Cook over low heat stirring constantly until the mixture has melted. Turn the heat to medium and cook without stirring for 5 minutes until it reaches the soft ball stage (a bit of the mixture will form a soft ball when added to ice water). Beat the egg in a small bowl and then add a few tablespoons of the chocolate mixture, mixing until smooth. Add this to the remaining chocolate and stir over low heat and then cook without stirring for 3 or 4 minutes or until it glazes the spoon. Remove from the heat and add the vanilla. Cool to room temperature. Heat the jam in a small saucepan over low heat until it melts. Spread jam evenly over one layer of the cake. Cover with the second layer. Pour the glaze evenly over the top layer and smooth with an offset spatula. Let stand until it stops dripping and then refrigerate for several hours. Bring to room temperature before serving. Serve with freshly whipped barely sweetened cream.

Pat and Peter, 1975

Peter's parents were both Jewish but in a very different way than my parents were. We did not belong to a synagogue but celebrated the holidays and had very deep ties to the land of Israel. Peter's parents, on the other hand, were founding members of Larchmont Temple but only went on the High Holidays, and it was only his father who participated. They were definitely Jewish in that all their friends were Jewish, and they ate many Jewish foods, but they did not practice Judaism and even celebrated Christmas.

My grandmother, Nana, was horrified, that the Gales held an annual Christmas party with a Christmas tree and a blue Santa on the front door. Nana told me that putting Santa on the front door was the worst of it, because it fooled the world into thinking that they were Christians, and that was denying their heritage. Nana once asked Pat why she celebrated Christmas and Pat answered that it was not a religious holiday but an American one. Nana replied that she should celebrate it on any other day but Christ's birthday.

The Gales were famous for their parties, but the most talked about party of the year was their Christmas Day Open House. They treated their guests to hors d'oeuvres, such as shrimp cocktail, smoked salmon, and all sorts of things that I would not eat—like caviar on little pieces of white bread, which I learned were called canapes. Pat actually prepared the canapes herself, and I felt very embarrassed about not indulging in them, but I just could not bring myself to eat caviar, and I still have never tasted it.

Although Pat and Ed were famous among their many friends for these parties, I am not sure that Pat enjoyed the parties as much as Ed did. Pat always made her appearance almost half way through the party, leaving the rest of us to entertain the company. Ed spent much of the time concocting and serving his infamous eggnog. This was yet another never-before-tasted *goyishe* (non-Jewish) concoction for me.

Ed's eggnog was infamous due to its sneaky intoxicating properties, which Peter just now told me was the addition of rye to the usual rum, which Ed would add to cut the sweetness. It was thick, sweet, and topped with globs and globs of freshly whipped clouds of cream. I literally drained my cup in a few delicious gulps, which was not a good thing! I truly had never tasted rum, let alone rye, before that, and I was so dizzy I had to go upstairs and lie down to recuperate. It took me many years before I could drink it again, and by then the number of calories per cup were way too many!

My parents grew up in kosher homes, so out of the need to rebel and fit in with their American friends they rejected the foods of their childhood. Yes, we had bagels and a few other traditional foods, such as challah bread on Friday night and potato pancakes on Hanukkah, but day-to-day food in my house was nearly always international gourmet. Brisket, stuffed cabbage, and matzo ball soup were made by my grandmothers, not by my mother.

On the other hand, Peter's family enjoyed a traditionally Jewish meal every now and then, and stuffed derma or *kishke* was one of their favorites. I don't know why, but this savory treat that is very much like stuffing was never served in my house. It is probably because the idea of serving stuffed intestines (the original recipe), was not something my mother would ever choose to do. I just realized that we never had any kind of stuffing (Aunt Roda made her Ritz Cracker stuffing for Thanksgiving), so it must have been a calorie thing for my mother.

Stuffed derma was originally vegetables and crackers or matzo meal that was stuffed into intestines; that's what kishke means. I am sure that I never would have ordered it at a Jewish deli because it sounds so dreadful! It is sliced, sautéed until crisp and then drowned in brown gravy. Ed adored it and encouraged me to try it, which I did, and I loved it and I still do (calories be damned). It is comfort food and makes you feel all warm and cozy in your tummy.

STUFFED DERMA

INGREDIENTS

1 box saltine or Ritz crackers or matzo meal
2 celery stalks
4 oz. vegetable oil or chicken fat
2 carrots
1 large onion
1 tsp. paprika
Salt and black pepper

DIRECTIONS

Put all ingredients in a food processor and mix until smooth. Shape into a roll and encase in aluminum foil. Bake at 375° for 45 minutes.

While in many ways Peter's family was very similar to mine, there were many aspects of their family life that felt very foreign to me. Perhaps the biggest difference was the atmosphere at the dinner table. In my home, my father demanded dinner the moment he walked in the door, which changed daily with his schedule at the hospital and his office hours. This was certainly a challenge for my mom, who truly created a wonderful meal every night. It is very difficult to have a complex dinner, such as Beef Stroganoff, ready at a moment's notice, but she did it.

My father ate a piece of pastry for breakfast, perhaps a piece of fruit for lunch, and he often did not get home for dinner until well past eight. We were able to wait for him because my mother would give us snacks like cheese and crackers or carrots and celery to hold us. However, my father would come home as hungry as a bear and sit down and devour his meal. Platters of food were laid on the table, and we served ourselves. After he finished everything on his plate, he would then clean our plates as well. Dinner was done in a matter of minutes, and conversation was kept to a bare minimum, as my father was in no mood for chit-chat.

When my father finished eating, he would leave the table and go to his bedroom to read his medical journal. He never even attempted to help clear the table—that job was left to us. Our live-in housekeeper was in the kitchen all through dinner and never entered the dining room. My brother was a "picky eater," according to my parents, which was fine during the day when he was permitted to eat whatever he wanted. However, at dinner he was expected to eat what was served. My father insisted that we had to eat what was on our plates, and we were not permitted to leave the table until we had done so. My trick was to put whatever I would not eat up my sleeve without being detected. Apparently, this edict of my father's did not end well for my brother, and according to my mom, my brother was forced to sit at the table for long periods of time until he was able to leave for one reason or another.

Dinnertime at the Gale household was an entirely different scene. Their housekeeper was also the cook, who had a regular schedule of meals to make that consisted of roast beef, fried chicken, meat loaf, etc.—repeated on a weekly basis. Food was served by the housekeeper, who brought the extra food back to the kitchen. There were buzzers on the floor to step on to call the housekeeper for second helpings. Dinner was served every evening at 8:00 p.m. on the dot, and it was an elegant, lengthy, and very loud affair. The Gales were very vocal about politics and current events, and conversations were spiked with raised voices shooting back and forth across the table. This was so entirely different from my upbringing that I never got used to it. Even when we lived at their house (story to follow in a later chapter), I was never comfortable at their table.

This is not to say that I was comfortable at my parents' table either, but it was a very different kind of discomfort. One meal that Peter and I both had to suffer through was beef tongue! (It was so awful to see that big, fat tongue staring at you!) This was when I ultimately used my sleeve trick to hide the food. Peter drowned his with mustard in order to swallow it. He could barely tolerate vegetables as well, which were canned or frozen. His technique was to crowd all the vegetables onto his spoon and swallow them in one big gulp!

We ate a lot of vegetables in my house—not the usual kind—that my friends had never seen or tasted before, and it was a great treat to introduce my friends to artichokes, peas in the pod, okra, and eggplant. One of my favorite eggplant recipes is *Baba Ghanoush*, which Peter had never tasted before when we were first dating. I had offered to cook for a fundraising auction at school, so I prepared an authentic Middle Eastern meal with baba ghanoush, hummus, shish kebab, and couscous. The meal raised a nice amount of money, and I introduced Peter, who assisted me for the first time, to smokey, creamy, marvelous baba ghanoush!

BABA GHANOUSH

INGREDIENTS

2 large eggplants, halved
   lengthwise, sprinkled with 1
   Tbs. kosher salt
1/2 cup tahini paste
Juice from 2 lemons
1/4 cup parsley, chopped
2 garlic cloves, minced
1 tsp. fresh mint, chopped or
   1/2 tsp. dried mint
Paprika
Salt and pepper
Olive oil

DIRECTIONS

Preheat oven to 450°. (You may also preheat a grill.) Allow the eggplants to sit in a colander in the sink for half an hour and then rinse. Cook the eggplants on the grill until they are black all over (about 20 minutes) and they have collapsed completely. Alternatively, you can char the eggplants on top of a gas stove and then continue to roast in the oven, which should take another half hour or so. Using a large metal spoon, scrape the flesh from the skin and place in a wooden bowl. Chop finely by hand with a metal chopping blade. In a small bowl, combine the tahini, garlic, half the lemon juice, and 1 Tbs. of water, mixing well with a fork. Add this mixture to the eggplant, seasoning to taste with salt, pepper, and additional lemon juice, if desired. Place in a serving dish and sprinkle with mint, paprika, parsley, and olive oil. Serve with pita, crackers, or crudités.
SERVES 6

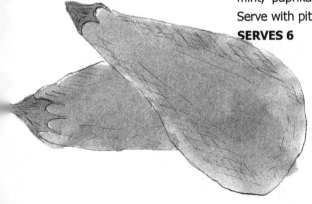

The first cookbook I ever bought was from the Connecticut College bookstore, during my freshman year. It was titled, <u>MMMMMM</u>, and was the first book published by the then-unknown author, Ruth Reichl. It was sweet, personal, adorably illustrated—and I have been cooking from it ever since. I went to a lecture by Ms. Reichl about fifteen years ago; she signed my copy and said that she couldn't believe that there was still a copy of the book out in the world. She lives very close by to us now, and I see her in the supermarket and the greenmarket quite often. I first made her recipe for *Funghi* (Mushroom) *Trefollati* in the shared kitchen of my freshman dormitory and have loved it every time I make it. I could literally have that, alone, for dinner with a crusty baguette

FUNGHI TREFOLLATI ALLA RUTH

INGREDIENTS

2 Tbs. olive oil
2 Tbs. unsalted butter
1 lb. cultivated mushrooms, quartered
2 shallots, minced
1 garlic clove, minced
1 lemon
1 Tbs. fresh parsley, chopped
Salt and black pepper

DIRECTIONS

Heat the oil and butter in a large sauté pan until the butter has begun to sputter. Add the mushrooms, shallot, and garlic and cook until the mushrooms have softened. Turn off the heat and squeeze the lemon over the mixture and sprinkle with the parsley. Season to taste and serve hot.

SERVES 2–4

I cooked this and many other dishes in the little kitchen down the hall in the dorm. I don't think there was more than a single pot, knife, and wooden spoon in there, but that did not deter me from preparing the most "gourmet" meals that I could imagine. After a summer trip to Montreal and Quebec City, I returned to school in the fall and tried to recreate some of the dishes we had tasted on our wonderful eating adventure. We tried a classic Québecois dessert of freshly made white bread covered with maple sugar and doused with heavy cream that was so rich, so sweet, and so good! Just thinking about it now puts my teeth on edge, but at the time we polished it off without a second thought.

One night in Montreal we went to a Russian restaurant that was dark, exotic, and very romantic. The couple at the table next to us was an older conservative-looking man in his seventies with a scantily-dressed young woman. After dinner, Peter remarked about the call girl next to us; I was completely clueless about it— much too focused on my dinner to take notice. I had ordered my first Chicken Kiev and was so far transported to butter heaven to be aware of anything except the melted butter that was literally pouring from inside the breaded chicken.

I tried unsuccessfully to recreate the Chicken Kiev in that little dorm kitchen, but the butter escaped into the oil in which I sautéed the chicken. A few years ago, I taught a Russian cooking class, and once again, it was an almost impossible task to keep the butter inside the chicken, but I think one or two of my students succeeded.

CHICKEN KIEV

INGREDIENTS

1 stick butter

1 tsp. fresh lemon juice

1 tsp. fresh tarragon or chives, finely chopped

2 tsp. fresh parsley, finely chopped

1 tsp. sea salt

Freshly ground black pepper, to taste

4 chicken cutlets

2 eggs, beaten

All-purpose flour

2 cups fresh bread crumbs

Wooden skewers

Vegetable oil for frying

DIRECTIONS

Using the metal blade of a food processor, or in a small bowl with a fork, combine the butter, lemon juice, tarragon or chives, parsley, salt, and pepper until smooth and form into 4 cylinders. Place each piece of chicken between two pieces of plastic wrap on a work surface and, using a meat pounder, carefully flatten the breast without tearing the meat. Then wrap the butter pieces in each chicken cutlet, tucking in the sides so that it resembles an envelope. Use the wooden skewers to secure, if necessary. Refrigerate for 1–2 hours, if possible. Roll the chicken in the flour, then the egg, and then the bread crumbs, making sure that the chicken cutlets are thoroughly covered with bread crumbs. Heat enough oil in a large frying pan so that it comes up about 2 inches in the pan. Heat until the oil reaches 360 ° on a deep-frying thermometer. Fry the cutlets until they are golden brown on all sides. Drain and serve at once.

SERVES 4

Peter and I understood very early on in our relationship that going out for a meal was our favorite type of date, and we made a regular practice of eating at restaurants in the New London area. However, there weren't many places worthy of remembering.

One of the few dishes that I truly enjoyed was at a rather fancy Greek restaurant along the port of New London. I recall that there was a banana importing company right next door to the restaurant, which I thought was very peculiar. This was one of the fancier places we went to, and I believe that it must have closed after our freshman year, because we never went back. They served a roast chicken with lemon, garlic, and oregano that was juicy, crispy, and never overcooked. My mouth is literally watering right now as I describe the dish.

LEMON CHICKEN

INGREDIENTS

1 chicken, cut into 8 pieces
3 lemons
2 Tbs. fresh oregano
1 onion, sliced thinly
Flour
Sea salt and black pepper
Vegetable oil

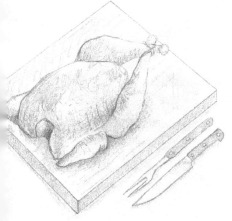

DIRECTIONS

Preheat the oven to 375°. Juice the lemons and rub the chicken all over with the juice, add the oregano (you may use 4 Tbs. of dried oregano), and allow to marinate at room temperature for about an hour. Season the flour with the salt and pepper. Dredge the chicken in the flour. Cover the bottom of a frying pan with the oil and place over moderate heat. When the oil is hot, add the onions and the chicken, and brown the chicken on all sides. Remove the chicken and the onions to a baking sheet with sides that has been covered with parchment paper. Place in the oven and cook for about 30 minutes or until the juices that run when poked with a knife are clear.

SERVES 4

I grew up eating fantastic Chinese food in Manhattan's fascinating Chinatown. My father understood very early on that this is a complex and wondrously varied cuisine. Peter, on the other hand, had only eaten the Cantonese food that most Americans think of as Chinese food: wonton soup, chow mein, fried rice, etc. However, he was a very eager student when I brought him to much more authentic Chinese restaurants: Szechuan, Hunan, Peking, and so on.

One time while we were visiting my parents on Long Island, I took Peter to a Szechuan restaurant in Hicksville, of all places! We had an unforgettable dish called Ants Climbing Trees, which I think is the absolutely best name! The noodles are the trees and the pork are the ants. It is the Chinese version of Spaghetti Bolognese. It is made with just a few ingredients but has a very broad range of flavors and textures, so delicious! It is made with clear mung bean vermicelli noodles with bits of ground pork clinging to them, which sounds nasty but is the stuff of my dreams. Really! I have made this again and again and have never been able to duplicate the complexity of flavors, but it is still very yummy and my go-to comfort food.

Back to the restaurant in Hicksville; although the food was amazing, the rice that came with our food was mushy and overcooked, so I sent it back to the kitchen. The chef came charging out of the kitchen holding his cleaver over his head. We surmised that he wanted to know who sent the rice back, so we ate our dinner as quickly as we could, paid the bill, and never went back!

ANTS CLIMBING TREES

INGREDIENTS

4 oz. Chinese dried bean thread noodles

2 tsp. sesame oil

3 Tbsp. canola oil

4 oz. ground pork

4 cloves garlic, minced

1 3-inch piece of ginger, peeled and minced

3 Tbsp. *doubanjiang* (Chinese red chili bean paste)

1/2 tsp. five-spice powder

2 Tbsp. light soy sauce

3 tsp. Chinese rice wine

1 1/2 cups chicken stock

2 Tbsp. dark soy sauce

3 *suan miao* (Chinese chives, blossoms discarded) or scallions, thinly sliced

DIRECTIONS

Place noodles and 4 cups boiling water in a bowl; let sit until soft, about 4 minutes. Drain and toss noodles with sesame oil and set aside. Heat canola oil in a large wok over medium-high heat. Add pork and cook, breaking up meat, until browned, about 5–7 minutes. Add garlic and ginger. Cook, stirring until fragrant, about 1 minute. Add paste, 5-spice powder, light soy, wine, and stock—and bring to a boil. Add noodles and cook 8–10 minutes more, stirring occasionally, until liquid is reduced by half, and stir in dark soy and chives.

The absolutely hands-down, best Chinese restaurant ever was a subterranean dive in Manhattan's Chinatown on Mott Street, called King Wu. It was so authentic that when we went there, from the time I was a child of eight or nine, we were usually the only non-Asians in the restaurant. It was such a dive that Nana not only refused to use their bathroom (not an unusual thing for her), but forbade us to use it as well. The second most embarrassing thing about going there with my dad was that before he would order, he would walk up and down the restaurant to see what everyone was eating in order to find the next best dish for us to try.

But the most embarrassing thing was that often these sweet people would offer him a taste of what they were eating, and he would always take them up on the offer. Looking back, it all seems very daring and adventurous and, I must say, endearing! But at the time, I wanted to melt right into the worn-out cushions of the booth where we sat.

It was here in the 1960s that I first tried hot and sour soup, mu shu pork, and watercress with garlic. But the very best dish they made, which I have not ever encountered again, was stuffed fish in bean-curd skin. The fish was ground and held together with egg white, as in fancy French *quenelles* or simple Jewish *gefilte* fish. However, these fish dumplings were not served naked and slimy, they were enrobed in paper-thin sheets of bean-curd skin that were then deep-fried to form the crispiest, yet lightest, most extravagant dish ever to be dipped in a vinegar-based sauce that was the perfect contrast to their oily richness! Here is as close as I can get to the original.

STUFFED FISH IN BEAN-CURD SKIN

INGREDIENTS

1/2 lb. fresh white fish
(flounder, sole, cod, etc.),
ground
1/4 cup water chestnuts, finely
chopped
1/4 cup bamboo shoots,
shredded
8 dried shitake mushrooms,
soaked in warm water
2 Tbs. tamari
1 Tbs. freshly grated ginger
1 Tbs. hoisin sauce
2 tsp. five-spice powder
1 tsp. toasted sesame oil
1 tsp. corn starch
1 egg, lightly beaten
4 sheets fresh tofu sheets, or
dried tofu sheets soaked in
warm water until soft
Vegetable oil for frying
Ponzu sauce for dipping

DIRECTIONS

In a medium bowl combine the fish, water chestnuts, bamboo shoots, and mushrooms. Add the ginger, tamari, hoisin, 5-spice powder, sesame oil, corn starch, and egg—and mix well. Depending on the size of the tofu sheets, use them whole, halved, or quartered so that once rolled up they will be the size of a large egg roll. Place a tablespoon of the fish mixture on the wide edge of the tofu sheet close to you and roll up tightly, tucking in the sides to form a spring roll, moistening the farthest edge with water just before closing it up.

Heat to boiling a wok filled to come up one-third of the way with water and place a piece of parchment paper or a leaf of cabbage on the surface of the bamboo steamer. Add the rolls and cover and steam for 15 minutes. Remove to a clean dishtowel. Place enough oil in the clean wok to come up one third of the way and heat until the handle of a wooden spoon is surrounded by air bubbles when placed in the oil. Fry the tofu rolls on all sides until they are golden and crisp all over. Drain and serve hot with the ponzu sauce for dipping.
SERVES 4

I spent the summers during my college years working in my dad's office in Massapequa, which was pretty boring, as I spent most of my time putting away files. My father had thousands of patients, and there were no computers in those days—so everything was recorded on files, and there were rooms full of them. I did enjoy the women who worked for and idolized my dad and therefore were very sweet to me. My favorite was a wonderful Italian woman named Bea; I used to call her Bea-Bea. She loved to cook and bake, and we often talked about her favorite dishes. One day she invited my mom and me over to her house so she could teach us her cheesecake recipe.

It remains my absolute favorite cheesecake because—unlike Jewish-style New York cheesecake, which is so solid from all the cream cheese—this cake is light, airy, and fluffy. I adapted the original recipe for use at Passover by substituting crushed coconut macaroons for the graham cracker crust, and it remains my go-to dessert for Seder.

Peter and me in Woodbury, 1976

BEA'S ITALIAN (PASSOVER) CHEESECAKE

INGREDIENTS

9- or 10-inch spring-form pan, lightly buttered

All ingredients at room temperature

1 lb. cream cheese (two 8 oz. packages)

1 cup sugar

6 extra-large eggs, separated

2 cups sour cream

1 tsp. vanilla extract

1/2 tsp. cream of tartar

1 1/2 cups graham cracker crumbs (1 package), or 2 cups coconut macaroons, crushed

4 Tbs. butter, melted

1 1/2 tsp. cinnamon, ground

Strawberries and whipped cream

DIRECTIONS

Preheat oven to 425°. Combine graham cracker crumbs, butter, and cinnamon and firmly press into bottom and part way up the sides of the pan—or alternatively, press macaroon crumbs on bottom of pan. Refrigerate. Beat the cream cheese and sugar until sugar is dissolved. Gradually add the egg yolks one at a time, mixing well after each egg. Keep beating while adding the sour cream and vanilla, and mix well. In a separate bowl, beat the egg whites and cream of tartar until stiff. Fold into the cream cheese batter until no white shows. Place a roasting pan with 2 inches of boiling water on bottom rack. Pour batter into prepared pan and bake for 15 minutes on center rack. Lower the heat to 250° and bake for 50 minutes or until firm. Turn off the heat, open oven door part way and allow cake to cool in oven for one hour. Cover and refrigerate overnight. Remove from pan and serve with strawberries and whipped cream.

The first year I came to Peter's house for Rosh Hashanah, which was our sophomore year, Pat was very excited to present to me a "traditional" New Year's dish, *charoset*. Charoset is, in fact, traditional for Passover, not for Rosh Hashanah. In truth, they both contain apples as the main ingredient, and I am quite sure that I was not appropriately grateful for her cooking efforts.

CHAROSET

INGREDIENTS

6 peeled apples, coarsely chopped
2/3 cup chopped walnuts
3 Tbs. honey, or to taste
1/2 tsp. cinnamon
Juice of 1 lemon
4 Tbs. sweet red wine or grape juice

DIRECTIONS

Combine all, mixing thoroughly. Add wine or juice as needed. Blend to desired texture—some like it coarse and crunchy, others prefer it ground to a paste. Chill.
MAKES 3 CUPS

Although I had a pleasant experience at Connecticut College, it felt unfulfilling for two important reasons. The first was that I decided to become a Jewish Studies major within a Religious Studies Department which offered only a handful of relevant courses. Secondly, as a result of my relationship with Peter, I felt that I was regarded only as Peter's girlfriend, without any recognition as a person in my own right. I felt that I needed to get away but was not inclined to transfer schools, because I assumed that Peter and I would not continue if I were to be away permanently.

In the fall of our junior year, two of my friends suggested that I take the spring semester in Israel. This made a lot of sense to me in that I would be able to enhance my major and I had been to Israel and had friends there. I began studying at Tel Aviv University in the Overseas Program in January, 1977.

CHAPTER 4

TEL AVIV UNIVERSITY
JANUARY-JUNE 1977

My semester at Tel Aviv University began in a very cold and wet January. I had not packed properly, not knowing that Tel Aviv could ever be cold—so I arrived unprepared, without warm clothes or blankets. We had very good friends there who were like family and lent me everything I needed. I needed some time away to find myself after feeling completely ignored at college, and Tel Aviv was about halfway around the world away from school.

I lived in the student dorm, which housed eight students in four bedrooms, two bathrooms, common showers, and two small kitchens. The kitchen was located in the interior of the apartment, so there was no window in this kitchen. There were few dining facilities on campus, and the few that existed were very far from the dormitories. Therefore, we were required to make our own meals, and it was the first time that I was responsible for cooking for myself. It was a real challenge in many ways, but the hardest part was that we were learning intensive Hebrew and were not permitted to use English, even when shopping at the markets.

The local supermarket was just fine, and I shopped there most days, but it was the outdoor market, which was two bus rides away at the other end of Tel Aviv, that was the most wonderful place I had ever shopped. It is called the Carmel Market and is still my favorite outdoor market anywhere. After two bus rides home, the tomatoes were always crushed, and I was sure that I had overpaid for most of what I had bought, but it had been absolutely thrilling to bargain in Hebrew for my vegetables.

Israelis literally live on salads and consume them at least three times daily. The ubiquitous Israeli Salad is a combination of mostly tomatoes, cucumbers, peppers, and whatever else looks good at the market dressed with olive oil and lemon. Restaurants in Israel are made or fail based on the freshness of this iconic salad. Everyone develops his or her own ratio based on preference and availability. Here is mine:

ISRAELI SALAD

INGREDIENTS

1 tomato
1 cucumber
1 scallion
1 green pepper
1 red pepper
3 radishes
1/4 cup parsley
1 lemon
1/4 cup olive oil
1/4 cup tahini, thinned with 3
   Tbs. water—optional
Sea salt and freshly ground
   black pepper

DIRECTIONS

Wash and cut all the vegetables into bite-size pieces. Put into a bowl and dress with the lemon juice, olive oil, tahini sauce (if using), sea salt, and pepper, to taste. Serve promptly.

SERVES 2

My roommate at Tel Aviv University, Denise, was also from Long Island. She was very observant and ate only kosher food and did not travel on Shabbat. The eight of us sharing the kitchen had agreed to prepare only dairy food in the kitchen, because we did not have to have two sets of dishes, which keeping kosher would require if we were preparing both meat and dairy. Honestly, I was not very keen on giving up meat, and I remember a few times when I purposely made a meat meal just to spite my roommate. That seems pretty petty to me now, but I was not feeling very loyal to the cause.

The local butcher was unlike any I had seen at home. For instance, if you were buying half a delicious rotisserie chicken, you were asked if you wanted the top half or the bottom half. I had never heard of this! One day he had a big slice of lamb neck for sale and I was intrigued by this and brought it back to the dorm to prepare a dish from a Yemeni cookbook I had bought—lamb-neck soup! You can just imagine the look on my roommate's face when she looked into the pot!

YEMENITE LAMB-NECK SOUP

INGREDIENTS

2 lb. lamb neck, cut into 2-inch pieces
2 quarts beef or chicken stock
1 onion, chopped
3 carrots, peeled and chopped
2–3 Tbs. tomato paste
2–3 Tbs. *hawayej* (Yemeni spice mix or curry powder)
1 bunch parsley, chopped
3 medium russet potatoes, peeled and chopped
Sea salt and freshly ground black pepper, to taste

DIRECTIONS

Place the lamb neck and stock in a large soup pot and bring to a boil. Lower the heat to medium and skim any foam off the top and discard. Add the onion, carrots, tomato paste, spice mix, and parsley. Boil for 2–3 hours or until thoroughly cooked. Add the potatoes and the salt and pepper and cook an additional half hour or until the potatoes are cooked through. Season to taste.

SERVES 6

The life at the student dorm was bearable, but I never would have made it through the semester if it had not been for my family's dearest friends, the Herolds. The dad, Henry, and my dad were residents together at Brooklyn Jewish Hospital before I was born, and they became instant BFFs. The mom, Annie, who was born in France and decided to make *aliyah* (immigration to Israel) when she was eighteen years of age, was there for me whenever I needed it.

The Herolds have three children, including a son, Ariel, who is two years younger than I and one of my closest friends to this day, fifty years after we met. They also have two daughters: Daphna, who is four years younger than I; and Iris, the youngest, who was three years old when I first met the family when I came to Israel for the first time with a Jewish youth group.

Me, Daphna, Iris, and Annie

Annie arrived in Israel from France and asked what the new country needed most—and was told *psychologists*, so that is what she became. Today, at eighty-five, she continues to work as a volunteer in one of the high schools. Like many French women, she is very proficient in the kitchen, albeit somewhat reluctantly. When I was a student, I was so grateful for her delicious home-cooked meals. One day she whipped up a chocolate torte that was extraordinary. I had never tasted a flourless cake and the dense, not too sweet, complex flavor was unforgettable. Being flourless is what defines a torte as opposed to a cake.

ANNIE'S CHOCOLATE TORTE

INGREDIENTS

Nonstick spray
6 Tbs. butter
12 oz. semisweet chocolate
  chips
5 eggs, separated
10 Tbs. sugar
1/2 tsp. vanilla extract

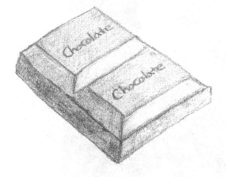

DIRECTIONS

Preheat oven to 350°. Using popover pans or deep cupcake tins, spray thoroughly with nonstick spray. Melt the butter and chocolate in a metal bowl over boiling water until smooth. Mix the egg yolks and 6 Tbs. of sugar in the bowl of an electric mixer on medium speed until it is pale yellow and very thick (about 5 minutes), adding the vanilla at the end. Stir in the chocolate mixture to combine. Place the mixture into a very large bowl. Into the clean bowl of the mixer, place the egg whites and beat until foamy. Add the rest of the sugar and beat until it forms stiff peaks. Fold the egg whites into the chocolate mixture until no white can be seen. Fill the tins about halfway and bake about 25 minutes, or until the centers are set but still soft.

SERVES 6

Annie filled an empty space in my life that spring. My mother had been sadly absent in my life for about five years, and Annie was interested and caring and available. She invited me to their home often and took me on outings to the antiques bazaar in Jaffa; to visit her son, Ariel, in his first year in the Army; and to visit friends in Tel Aviv and family in Jerusalem.

One of Annie's cousins from France, who lived in Jerusalem, owned a successful *foie gras* business that marketed their kosher goose-liver products in France. One weekend, Ariel and I took a cab to Jerusalem to stay with them in their fancy home on one of the beautiful hilltops overlooking the city. Walking around the Old City of Jerusalem, we stopped for lunch at an Arab restaurant, and I had my first taste of a peasant dish of beans with garlic and olive oil that is served at almost every meal; it is called *ful*. It doesn't sound like something one would crave, but it definitely is.

OLD CITY FUL

INGREDIENTS

1/2 lb. small dried fava beans
3 garlic cloves, crushed with 1 tsp. sea salt
1/4 cup extra-virgin olive oil
2 lemons
1/2 cup parsley, chopped
Sea salt and freshly ground black pepper
1 medium tomato, chopped
2 or 3 scallions, thinly sliced

DIRECTIONS

Wash the beans and cover them with cold water to soak overnight. Pick through the beans, discarding any that float, and rinse the rest. Place the beans in a deep pot or pressure cooker and cover with water by an inch. If using a deep regular pot, bring to a boil and then lower the heat and, partially covered, cook at a simmer for about two hours, adding water as needed until they are cooked through. If using a pressure cooker, follow the directions for cooking beans. Then add about a teaspoon of salt and allow the beans to cool. When ready to serve, cook the beans until they have absorbed most of the water and then add the garlic, the juice of one of the lemons, and half of the olive oil. Crush half of the beans, then add the parsley, salt, and pepper—and taste for seasoning. Plate the beans and garnish with the rest of the olive oil, tomatoes, scallions, and slices of the second lemon. Serve with fresh pita bread.

SERVES 4–6

Ariel and I spent the weekend seeing the Old City, walking through the ancient corridors that divide the area into Jewish, Armenian, Arab, and Christian quarters. I felt so many emotions all at once as we trekked through them all: excitement, awe, fear, disgust (the odors can be really intense!), delight (the markets had some of the very best local food)—as well as gratitude and a distinct sense of history and my place in it. Within a second flat, Jerusalem, literally the City of Peace, can disarm you through your admiration of an ancient synagogue (or mosque or church)—and then gainsay that awe around the turn of a corner by way of the insistent and somewhat menacing beckoning of a salesperson in the Souk.

Old City Souk, 1977

I never felt at home in the Arab Quarter, but I fell in love with its exoticism and intoxicating assault on all the senses. Arab hospitality is at its peak in the restaurants, where ten or twelve small salads (mezze) are at the table before you even order something to drink. They are always fresh and delicious and are refilled as you empty them. The trick is to hold back because you must order a main dish or there will be a real problem.

I discovered two new dishes at one of these wonderful restaurants that had low tables, Persian carpets, brass lamps, and colorful wall hangings. The first one is called *Chicken Musakhan*, which has absolutely nothing to do with Greek *moussaka*, which is an eggplant and lamb casserole. This Arab recipe is a simple but succulent peasant dish with chicken, onions, pita bread, and a plentiful amount of a seasoning called sumac, which is lemony and fragrant and a little spicy. It is not related to poison sumac, luckily, and adds deep flavor to every dish it is used in, such as soup, stew, salad, and hummus.

CHICKEN MUSAKHAN

INGREDIENTS

2 3-lb. organic chickens, quartered—or 4 Cornish Hens, halved
1/3 cup extra-virgin olive oil
6 large onions, sliced
1/2 cup ground sumac
3/4 cup pine nuts
1 tsp. ground allspice
1/4 tsp. ground cloves
1/4 tsp. ground cinnamon
4 large pita breads, halved
Salt and freshly ground black pepper

DIRECTIONS

Preheat oven to 450°. Heat half of the oil in a large sauté pan over medium-low heat. Add the onions and sauté until lightly golden. Season the chickens with the salt and pepper. Place the onions on the bottom of a large baking pan and arrange the chicken on top. Bake for 10 minutes and then reduce the temperature to 375° and bake another 20 minutes. For Cornish hens, bake 10 minutes.

Meanwhile, heat a small amount of the olive oil in the sauté pan and quickly toast the pine nuts. Remove from the heat and add the spices. Take the chicken from the oven and sprinkle the pine-nut mixture over the top and drizzle with the rest of the olive oil. Bake another 30 minutes or until juices run clear. If using Cornish hens, bake only another 10–15 minutes. To serve, place a piece of pita on each plate and top with a quarter of the chicken and a tablespoon or two of the onions and place under the broiler for a few moments, if desired.

SERVES 8

The other dish that I first enjoyed in East Jerusalem is called *Imam Bayildi*, which means the Imam (religious leader) fainted. There are many stories told to explain this curious name; one version is that the dish was so delicious it made the Imam faint. Another is that the garlic did him in, but my favorite is that he fainted because the dish used so much expensive olive oil. The dish is so special because the eggplant becomes very tender and takes on the perfume of the garlic, onion, pine nuts, tomatoes, and all that luscious olive oil. I could very happily have this for dinner with some pita, cucumbers, feta, and olives—done!

IMAM BAYILDI

INGREDIENTS

8 small Italian eggplants

1/2 cup olive oil

Sea salt

1/2 large onion, sliced thinly in half circles

2 garlic cloves, pressed

2 large tomatoes, chopped

2 Tbs. pine nuts

4 Tbs. fresh parsley, finely chopped

Sea salt and black pepper

DIRECTIONS

Preheat the oven to 375°. Using a vegetable peeler, cut three strips lengthwise down each eggplant. Rub them with the olive oil and sprinkle with salt. Place in a large baking pan and cover tightly with aluminum foil and bake for about 1 hour or until very soft and cooked through. While the eggplants are in the oven, sauté the onion and garlic in the remaining oil in a small pan and cook over moderate heat until softened. Add the tomatoes with the salt and pepper and cook for about 5 minutes or until the juice thickens. Turn off the heat and add the pine nuts, parsley, salt, and pepper. Cut a deep pocket into each eggplant, but do not cut through the bottom, and stuff them with the onion-tomato mixture. Pour over them any tomato juices in the pan and serve warm, cold, or at room temperature.

SERVES 4–8

Ariel's two sisters were much younger than I was, so we didn't really connect. The older one, Daphna, has become a dear friend over these many years, but in those days, we really didn't have much in common. At our first meeting at their beach house in Ashkelon when she was just thirteen, she invited me to play *matkot*. It is the Israeli game played on the beach with two wooden paddles and a small rubber ball that gets madly smacked back and forth, as quickly as possible. It was clear pretty soon that I was no match for her, as she was an Israeli who played the game often and she was very athletic. If you ever go to the beach in Israel, you will see matkot players up and down the beach, hitting the balls at breakneck speed, and you must be very careful not to get in their way, because they reign supreme!

At the time, the one thing Daphna and I had in common was a love for good food and how to make it. One evening her mom, Annie, told her to make a plum tart from the bushel of plums that one of her husband's Palestinian patients had given them. Daphna was then perhaps sixteen or seventeen. She began putting together the crust for this wonderful tart. I had never seen a crust that was pressed into a tart shell immediately, without being rolled out. Instead, the newly formed dough is put directly into the pan and pushed to the edges. It is a classic French *pâté sucrée*, but it was the first one I had ever eaten right out of the oven. It was swooningly delicious; the combination of sweet, buttery crust, dead-ripe plums and rich crème fraîche (another new taste) was truly transportive. I have since had dinner at Daphna's on many occasions, and I am never disappointed, which is saying a lot!

PLUM TART

INGREDIENTS

1 unbaked pâte sucrée (recipe follows)

8–10 ripe plums, sliced

Crème fraîche, enough to coat the bottom of the tart shell

Granulated sugar

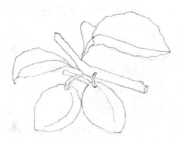

DIRECTIONS

Preheat the oven to 375°. Roll the pastry on a floured surface with floured rolling pins into circles that are 1 1/2 inches larger than your pastry tins. Place the pastry into the tin and trim the edges and decorate as desired. Spread the crème fraîche over the shell and then overlap the plum slices to cover the crème fraîche. Sprinkle all over with the granulated sugar. Bake for 35 minutes or until the top has browned.

Pâte Sucrée (sweet pastry)

Makes one crust for 9- or 10-inch tart

4 ounces (1 stick) unsalted butter, softened

1/3 cup sugar

1 egg yolk

1 1/2 cups pastry flour (not sifted)

1/2 tsp. salt

With an electric mixer or by hand, beat the softened butter and sugar until well blended. Beat in the egg yolk. Scrape down the sides of the bowl, then add the flour and salt all at once, mixing just until blended. Gather the dough together into a ball, then flatten to a disc and spread into a tart pan, spreading to the edges.

In addition to Annie and Henry, my parents had very good friends named Assaf and Nitza, who lived on a kibbutz in the Kinneret Valley near the Jordan River. A kibbutz is a community that farms communally and follows a community lifestyle. At that time, the parents did not sleep in the same home as their children, who lived together in a dormitory. This experimental way of living was designed to give the parents more time to work on the kibbutz and give the children a robust peer relationship. Children of the kibbutz system were known for their advancement in the army, due to their increased ability to form team bonds.

The families would gather every day after lunch for several hours of intense connection time, while giving parents and children more freedom the rest of the day. There is a wonderful book about this experiment called *The Children of the Dream* by Bruno Bettelheim. The homes had small kitchens designed for snacks and such, but not for meals, as all the members ate three meals a day at the central dining room. Everyone was given a job, either in the fields, central kitchen, laundry, school, or factory. Clothes were not privately owned but washed and distributed from the laundry.

Me and the Shafriri family

Our friends the Shafriri's had six children, which I imagine was only possible due to their parenting circumstances. This unusual set-up seemed to have worked out very well for them. Most kibbutzim (plural form) have altered the requirement for separating parents and children, as it must have been extremely difficult to maintain. However, while I was a student at Tel Aviv University I visited the family often and fully appreciated how Utopian this whole concept was. Their eldest daughter, Dalit, is my age, and we had a brief friendship at the time, and she visited us here in New York with five of their own six children.

Nitza and Dalit both enjoyed baking cakes and preparing snacks for guests in their miniature kitchen. One day, Dalit made these no-bake cookies when I came to visit. It is called "Chocolate Salami" because it really looks like salami when cut.

CHOCOLATE SALAMI

INGREDIENTS

5–6 oz. butter biscuits such as Petit Beurre
3/4 cup sliced almonds
1/2 cup unsalted butter at room temperature
1/2 cup superfine sugar
1/2 cup cocoa
1/4 cup egg whites
1 Tbs. dark rum
Powdered sugar for dusting/ rolling the salami
Optional: grated orange zest, chopped dried figs, dried currants, mini chocolate chips

DIRECTIONS

Place the biscuits into a sealable plastic bag and whack a few times with a rolling pin. Place in a large bowl and coarsely chop the sliced almonds and add to the bowl with the biscuits. Then cream together the butter and sugar, either by hand or in the food processor. Add the cocoa to the creamed mixture and blend well. Scrape the bowl and add the egg whites and extract/rum of your choice. Add to the bowl of the biscuits and chopped almonds and other optional ingredients, combining thoroughly to make your salami mix.

Remove the salami mix from the bowl onto a large piece of parchment paper and form into a log shape. Roll in the confectioner's sugar and cover with plastic wrap. Chill for two hours or until firm. Then dust/roll in powdered sugar again, slice thickly, and enjoy. Keep stored in the refrigerator. This may also be stored in the freezer for a great last-minute dessert.

SERVES 6

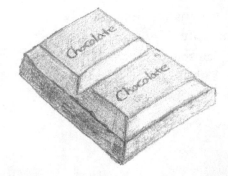

The grandmother of the family on the kibbutz was named Leah, and she came to Israel as a refugee from Eastern Europe. She brought her Old Country recipes with her and prepared homemade cheese blintzes for us one day. We all sat around the small table in their little house and ate and ate and ate until the grandmother was exhausted.

CHEESE BLINTZES

INGREDIENTS

Store-bought crêpes (or homemade)
8oz. package cream cheese, softened
1 cup small-curd cottage cheese
1 egg, beaten
1 Tbs. sugar
1 tsp. vanilla extract
Juice of half a lemon
1/4 tsp. ground cinnamon
Fruit preserves or frozen fruit, defrosted
3 Tbs. melted butter
Sour cream and/or confectioner's sugar, optional for topping

DIRECTIONS

Combine the cream cheese, cottage cheese, egg, sugar, vanilla and lemon juice in a small bowl. Preheat the oven to 350 degrees.

Place about 2 tablespoons of cheese filling on the bottom third of the pancake. If desired, add some preserves to the cheese filling. Fold in the sides and fold up the bottom of the pancake. Roll up to form a blintz. When all blintzes have been prepared, place in a buttered pan and top with the melted butter. Bake for 20 minutes or until the filling has solidified. Serve with the sour cream and/or confectioner's sugar, if desired.

SERVES 6

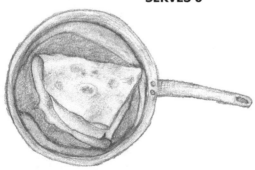

At the end of the semester, Peter came to visit me in Tel Aviv, and we traveled all over Israel together. I took him to many places that I knew well—the souk, the seashore, wonderfully exotic restaurants. Together, we discovered new places—the Dead Sea, Masada, and the amazing springs at Ein Gedi on the edge of the Negev Desert.

Peter at Ein Gedi

After traveling throughout Israel, we flew to Amsterdam and then to London. We had a great time experiencing all these new sights and tastes; and at the end of the trip, I arrived home with literally one dime in my pocket.

CHAPTER 5

5 SYCAMORE DRIVE
WOODBURY, NEW YORK
JUNE 1978-JANUARY 1980

Towards the end of college, I searched for a job in the Jewish art world because I was a Jewish Studies major with a minor in Art History. This seemed to me to be a logical, albeit small, parameter to search. During this process, unbeknownst to me, my father contacted an Israeli art dealer who lived on Long Island and with whom I had arranged an interview on my own. When I arrived at her home for the interview, she revealed to me that she was moving back to Israel and she would represent her artists through a gallery that I was opening with my father.

Connecticut College graduation photo, 1978

I was shocked, angry, embarrassed, humiliated—but also intrigued. I felt betrayed by my father, in that he had arranged all this behind my back. He, on the other hand, was thrilled to surprise me with a business. At twenty-two, I didn't feel ready for the responsibility of running a gallery, but I had no choice in this. My mother was to be my associate for the day-to-day routine, and my father was to foot the bills. As I write this, with a twenty-four-year-old daughter of my own I can see why this was exactly the opposite of what I had imagined for myself. In hindsight, I understand that my dad was trying to please me (and himself, I am certain) but this was too much–too fast, without my input, and destined for failure.

Mom and I took a class at Adelphi University on how to run an art gallery, which was reassuring because we seemed to be doing all the right things in terms of our advertising, publicity, and openings. I was writing all the publicity, designing the brochures, framing the paintings, and hanging the shows. I was even driving to Kennedy airport to pick up the artwork. For the opening of the gallery, I drove to Manhattan to escort the Israeli ambassador to the event. It was a great deal of responsibility and a huge learning curve.

Mom and I spent a lot of time together, which was mostly a good thing. We worked together—and because we lived together, we cooked together. One of the very best dishes I learned from her at that time was the crab cakes with remoulade recipe from the Southern cookbook in the Time/Life series.

CRAB CAKES WITH REMOULADE

INGREDIENTS

4 Tbs. butter
4 Tbs. flour
1 cup milk, warmed
Salt, black pepper, cayenne
1 lb. jumbo lump crabmeat,
  picked through for shells
1/4 cup fresh parsley, minced
3 scallions, minced
3 eggs, beaten
6–8 slices of French bread
  (made into breadcrumbs)
6 Tbs. butter
3 Tbs. vegetable oil
1 lemon
Remoulade sauce

Remoulade Sauce

1/4 cup Creole mustard (or
  substitute Pommery mustard)
  1/2 cup white wine vinegar
1 cup olive oil
4 scallions, chopped
1/2 cup parsley
1 Tbs. fresh tarragon (or 1 1/2
  tsp. dried)
1 Tbs. capers, drained
1 Tbs. sweet paprika
1 tsp. dried hot pepper powder
  1 Tbs. salt

DIRECTIONS

Heat a small saucepan over medium heat and add the 4 Tbs. of butter. When it starts to sizzle, add the flour. Stir until thickened and slowly add the milk and stir until it makes a thick sauce. Lower the heat and add the salt, pepper, and cayenne—and cook for a few minutes, then remove from the heat. In a medium-size bowl, add the crab, parsley, and scallions—and mix gently. Pour the sauce over the crab and blend. Refrigerate, if possible, for an hour.

Pour the eggs into a wide bowl. Place the bread crumbs into another wide bowl. Take the crab mixture and form into 3-inch flat disks. Dip these into the eggs and then the bread crumbs. Refrigerate the cakes for an hour, if possible. In a large sauté pan, heat the rest of the butter and the oil over medium-high heat. When the butter is sizzling, add the crab cakes and cook until nicely browned on the bottom. Carefully turn them over and brown on the other side. Serve with the lemon and remoulade sauce.

Place all the ingredients in the order listed into a blender. Blend until smooth and refrigerate until ready to serve.

SERVES 4–6

As sweet as it was for Mom and me to spend so much time together, all this closeness was pretty toxic for my relationship with Dad. He and I were both pretty opinionated and self-confident, which caused a lot of friction, especially when decisions needed to be made—and I knew that I was right, and he knew that he had the final say. We went on like this at the gallery and then had to go back home and act as though everything was fine. Cooking and baking were my only hobby and helped me occupy myself after work. My friends from high school were no longer around, and Peter was living in Manhattan with a friend from Westchester and working in New Jersey at his dad's factory. Peter was off weekends and would come to Long Island where I was working weekends. Needless to say, this was a challenging situation all around. My mom had taught me a great recipe for coconut brownies, which I often made when Peter was coming for a visit. They are still my favorite brownies!

COCONUT BROWNIES

INGREDIENTS

2 eggs, beaten
1 stick unsalted butter, melted
1 cup white sugar
1/2 cup white flour
1 tsp. baking powder
Pinch of salt
1/2 tsp. almond extract
1/2 cup sweetened shredded coconut
2 squares unsweetened chocolate

DIRECTIONS

Preheat oven to 350°. Butter an 8-inch square baking pan. Melt the chocolate in a double boiler and allow to cool. Combine the beaten eggs and the melted butter. Mix until smooth. Sift the flour, baking powder, and salt and add to the egg mixture. Remove 1/2 cup of the batter and add to it the almond extract and the coconut. Pour the melted chocolate into the bowl with the rest of the batter. Pour the chocolate batter into the pan and then drop the coconut batter by tablespoons on top of the chocolate batter, but do not spread it around. Bake about 30 minutes or until a toothpick comes out clean.

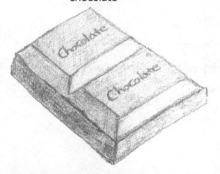

Peter and I did have some good times over that year and a half that we lived separately, but I think the most important piece of that time for me was that it confirmed that I was not happy when I wasn't with him. Our time off from our work was spent driving to each other. I visited Peter at his parents' home in Larchmont, and he came to see me in Woodbury. These were the days when women waited for men to ask to marry them—and never the other way around.

One day in the fall of 1978, we were walking along Long Island Sound in Manor Park in Larchmont when Peter went down on his knee and proposed. I knew that it was coming, but not when or where, and I was surprised and elated. We chose to wait until September of the next year to marry in my parent's backyard. I spent most of the summer of 1979 working in the gallery and planning the wedding.

The night before the wedding we had a rehearsal dinner at my parents' home, and I did most of the cooking, none of which I remember, except for the cake. It was a chocolate sauerkraut cake. It was very moist and delicious, and absolutely no one guessed the surprise ingredient, which feels like coconut in your mouth.

CHOCOLATE SAUERKRAUT CAKE

INGREDIENTS

2 cups all-purpose flour

1/2 cup high-quality cocoa
powder

1 tsp. baking powder

1 tsp. baking soda

1/4 tsp. sea salt

2/3 cup butter, softened

1 cup raw sugar

2 jumbo eggs

1 tsp. vanilla extract

1 cup water

1 cup sauerkraut, rinsed and
chopped

Chocolate Cream Cheese Frosting

2 oz. semisweet chocolate
chips, melted

8 oz. cream cheese, softened

3 tablespoons milk

2 cups confectioners' sugar

1/4 tsp. sea salt

1 teaspoon vanilla extract

DIRECTIONS

Preheat oven to 350°. In a medium bowl, whisk together flour, cocoa powder, baking powder, baking soda, and salt—and set aside. In a large bowl, cream together butter with sugar until light and fluffy. Add eggs one at a time, beating well after each addition. Beat in vanilla. Add the flour mixture in three stages alternately with the water, mixing well. Stir in the sauerkraut. Coat a 13 x 9-inch pan with cooking spray. Pour the batter into the pan and bake 35–45 minutes, until a toothpick tests clean. Let cool completely in pan. In a medium bowl, combine chocolate, cream cheese, milk, confectioners' sugar, salt, and vanilla with an electric mixer at high speed until smooth and creamy. Spread on cake.

I had been a vegetarian for the previous five years, so when I met with the caterer, I said that since it would be a hot day and this was going to be a luncheon, I would like a dairy meal. My father said that that was fine as long as we served roast beef and filet mignon! Oh, well! We started the meal with gazpacho, which was pretty unusual in those days and ended with a chocolate wedding cake—really unheard of!

Ed, Pat, Dad, Mom, Peter, me

We left for our honeymoon in France directly from the party with a list of all the restaurants that were a must, including a few reservations that we had made ahead of time. We had been told that we must go to Tour d'Argent for the pressed duck, which is still on the top recommendations for Paris. The waiter was describing in French all the sauces for the duck that were offered, and I thought I heard him say mushroom in French, which is *champignon*. I have always loved mushrooms, so that is what I ordered. The duck arrived with great ceremony and looked incredible until the waiter poured the thick, grey sauce on top. When I asked what the sauce was, he replied, "It is what you ordered, *rignon*—kidney!" I did not even taste it; Peter ate the entire duck!

Peter at the Eiffel Tower

We spent a week seeing all the popular sights and wandering through the unknown side streets and had a wonderful time. Then we rented a car and drove through the Loire Valley to our first stop, a chateau with our room in the turret. It was very picturesque and charming. We had dinner in the chateau next to a single older man with whom we conversed as much as my high school French would allow. Still feeling cheated over the mushroom sauce that I had missed in Paris, I ordered veal with mushrooms for dinner. The mushrooms were so strongly flavored with a slippery texture that I was nervous I might not survive the night. I now believe that they were porcini mushrooms, which I had never tasted before, but I don't think I ate more than two or three bites.

Me in the Loire Valley

VEAL MORENGO

INGREDIENTS

2 lbs. veal stew meat, cut into 2-inch pieces
1 Tbs. olive oil
1 medium yellow onion, finely diced
1 Tbs. all-purpose flour
Salt and black pepper
1 cup white wine
1 Tbs. fresh basil or tarragon
1 tsp. fresh thyme
3 medium tomatoes, chopped
1 cup fresh mushrooms, any variety, quartered
2 Tbs. crème fraîche

DIRECTIONS

Preheat the oven to 325°. Dry the veal pieces with a paper towel. Heat the oil over medium heat in an oven-proof pot. Brown the veal on all sides and season with salt and pepper. Add the onion and stir until the onion has softened. Add the flour and stir until it has been absorbed. Add the wine and stir until all the brown bits on the bottom of the pot have come loose. Add enough water so that the meat is submerged. Add the herbs, cover the pot and place into the oven for an hour and a half, stirring occasionally. Add the tomatoes and mushrooms and continue baking for another half an hour. Stir in the crème fraîche. Taste for seasoning. Serve over noodles or rice.

SERVES 4

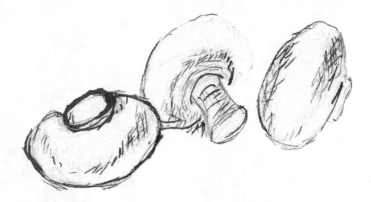

After touring the Loire Valley, we drove South to Roanne to eat lunch at the super famous, Les Frères Trois Gros. It was a prix fixe meal that cost $200 and was far beyond our budget but an absolute must for our honeymoon experience. The problem was that our reservation for lunch was at 1:00 p.m., and we arrived in Roanne at around 12:00, absolutely starving. So, we were forced to stop at a fantastic pastry shop next door to the restaurant and stuff ourselves with cream puffs before lunch.

This misguided move made it very difficult for me to have any appetite at all before our extravagant lunch. However, we sat and did our best to enjoy the lunch. And although I have not got the slightest clue what we ate, I will never forget what happened at the end of the meal. After at least two hours of sitting next to a small table to our right, the couple eating there got up to leave, and out from under the table emerged two very large Standard Poodles, who had been extremely quiet and well-behaved for all that time. It was so very French!

From there we drove to Avignon and stayed at a charming hotel right beside the famous bridge of Avignon that the song is about ("Sur la Pont d'Avignon"). We had dinner outside in the courtyard, and I tasted the soup the area is known for, *pistou*. Pistou is almost identical to pesto, as it is a paste of basil, nuts, cheese, and olive oil. This paste is added to a soup that is brimming with seasonal vegetables, such as zucchini, carrots, beans, and potatoes—all cut to the same exact size. It explodes with flavor and is just delicious.

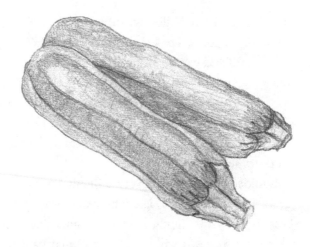

SOUPE AU PISTOU

INGREDIENTS

1 quart beef broth or water
1 carrot, peeled and diced
1 leek, cleaned and diced
2 tomatoes, diced
1 small new potato, diced
1 cup green beans, ends
  removed and sliced
1 yellow squash, diced
1 zucchini, diced
1/2 cup fine noodles
2 Tbs. fresh basil, torn into
  small pieces
2 garlic cloves, chopped
2 oz. freshly grated parmesan
  cheese
6 Tbs. extra-virgin olive oil
Salt and black pepper, to taste

DIRECTIONS

Bring beef broth plus 2 cups of water or 1 1/2 quarts of water to a boil in a large pot and add the vegetables up to the green beans, yellow squash and zucchini. Boil for 15 minutes, then add the remaining vegetables and boil 15 more minutes, then add the noodles and boil 10 more minutes, and remove from the heat. Cover the pot. In a mortar, crush the basil, garlic, and cheese and then add the olive oil drop by drop until it is all incorporated and smooth. Then add a spoonful of soup into the paste to thin it. Now stir the pistou into the broth and taste for seasoning.

SERVES 4–6

I was beginning to have trouble zipping my jeans, and so I ordered a salade Niçoise in Nice. My request of *sans anchois*, (without anchovies) was taken with a grimace from the waiter. Our dessert of wild strawberries, served with our first taste of crème fraîche, was swoonable. I then requested an additional drizzle of crème fraîche, and this was flatly denied. Ah, the French! From Avignon we drove to Provence to see the Joan Miro museum and had lunch in Aix-en-Provence in a Moroccan restaurant for an outstanding couscous with all the trimmings. I remember being so grateful for a meal that was not French cuisine.

Peter at the Miro Museum

At this point, we were both tired of fancy French cuisine and the stuffy atmosphere that goes along with it. This was a tiny restaurant in the middle of a very steep hill. It was packed for lunch with locals and we were happily squeezed into the middle of them. It was our first taste of a complete couscous meal, and it was exotic, tasty, and very cheap—an authentic ethnic meal after so much rich and snobby food.

LAMB WITH VEGETABLES AND COUSCOUS

INGREDIENTS

1 1/2 lbs. lamb stew meat
  (shoulder), cut into 2-inch
  pieces
3 Tbs. olive oil
1 medium onion, chopped
1 Tbs. tomato paste
1 turnip, cubed
1/2 cup green and red bell
  peppers, cut in 1-inch pieces
2 cloves garlic, minced
1 cup canned chickpeas,
  washed and drained
1 tomato, chopped
1 winter squash, peeled,
  seeded, cut in 1-inch cubes
1 tsp. ground cinnamon
1 tsp. ground cumin
1 tsp. turmeric
2 lemons
2 tsp. fresh or 1 tsp. dried mint
1/4 tsp. hot sauce
Salt and black pepper
Couscous, cooked according to
  package directions

DIRECTIONS

Heat half of the olive oil over medium heat in a large pot. Add the meat and cook, stirring occasionally until the meat is no longer pink. Add the onions and continue to cook for about 10 minutes or until the onions are beginning to brown. Add the tomato paste and the peppers and cook for 5 more minutes. Add 1 1/2 cups of water and bring to a boil. Cover and cook over low heat for about half an hour. Add the garlic, chickpeas, tomato, squash, and seasonings. Add enough water to just cover the mixture. Cook about 20 minutes or until the squash is tender. Add the juice from the lemons, the dried mint, hot sauce to taste, and salt and pepper as needed. Serve with couscous prepared according to directions on box.

SERVES 4–6

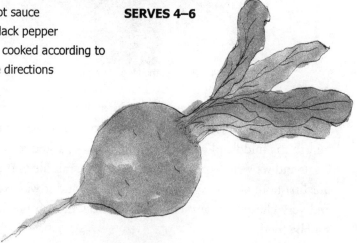

Our last stop of the honeymoon was in Haute-de-Cagnes, where we stayed in a very luxurious hotel, using all the extra money my father had given me as we left for the airport. Sitting across the dining room on our first evening was one of my most favorite actors, Gene Wilder. I was completely starstruck, but I needed to let him know that I was a fan, so I took a rose from the vase on the table and walked over and handed it to him, unable to utter a single word. He just stared at me with those huge eyes in bewilderment. I was so embarrassed but very glad that I made the connection, as goofy as it was.

We wandered around Provence—going to markets, visiting Nice and Monte Carlo, and truly enjoying the end of a beautiful time in France—ready to begin our life as a married couple in Peter's grandmother's apartment in Greenwich Village, which his parents had so generously given to us as a wedding present. Little did we know that this was going to be one of the most challenging times of our new marriage.

CHAPTER 6

70 EAST TENTH STREET
NEW YORK CITY
SEPTEMBER 1979-JANUARY 1983

We returned from our honeymoon and packed the few things we owned and brought them to the apartment in Greenwich Village where Peter's grandmother had lived in until her recent passing. It was filled with all her furniture, dishes, clothing, and (ugh!) bathroom items. Before it could become our own, we had to remove all her things—quite a big task! Typical New York City apartment; no window in the kitchen!

Around midnight of the first day, we heard a knock at the door. It was the building's handyman, who had been instructed to find out who we were. We tried to explain that we were Ann's grandson and wife and we were the new owners of the apartment. He informed us that that was impossible, as we had not been approved by the Board and that we needed to remove all our things in the morning and could not move in until and if we were approved. Peter's father clearly had no idea how Co-op Boards in New York City function. It was a deep blow!

We literally had nowhere to go and in the morning moved into Peter's parents' house in Larchmont. We expected to be there about a month, living in his old bedroom and commuting each day to New Jersey and Long Island. One month lasted six months until finally the Board agreed to interview us and then at last approve us. This was a very challenging time for us as newlyweds, because living in his childhood bedroom was very constricting, to say the least. The most difficult part of the experience for me was that they had a housekeeper who was also the cook, so the kitchen was off-limits, and we were expected for dinner at 8:00 p.m. in the dining room for whatever Doris had prepared for the meal.

Five months after being thrown out of 70 East Tenth Street, the Co-op Board finally agreed to interview us. During the interview, someone asked what the "density" level for the one-bedroom apartment was. We had no idea what that meant (I thought they might be talking about how many chairs could fit in it) but learned that they were concerned that we would be having children, which they sincerely did not want. The median age in the building was no less than seventy-five, and I think they saw us as a threat to the status quo. However, we were finally accepted and moved into the apartment in February 1980.

During the waiting time, we closed the Israeli art gallery on Long Island due to the intolerable stress it created for our family, and I took a job on Twenty-Third Street in the art collection department of an advertising and marketing company. I worked there cataloguing their artwork and serving as the "monkey" (raising my hand to bid on prechosen artwork) at the biggest art auction houses in Manhattan. It lasted six months until I decided that I needed a Master's degree in something in order to have a career where I was respected more than I was for the work for AdMar. However, I did love the excitement at the auctions, and Peter and I often attended them afterwards.

In January, we threw ourselves a party to celebrate finally

moving into the apartment and invited all our friends to a feast I prepared of pasta with three different sauces and dessert of several types of homemade ice cream. The *Bolognese* sauce for the pasta is still my go-to recipe but will definitely spoil you for any sauce you have at a restaurant.

SPAGHETTI BOLOGNESE

INGREDIENTS

2 Tbs. extra-virgin olive oil
2 Tbs. butter
1 small onion, diced
1 garlic clove, minced
1 carrot, diced
1 celery stalk, diced
1 lb. ground beef
1 cup white wine
1/2 cup milk
1 large can crushed tomatoes
1 Tbs. fresh basil
1 tsp. fresh or 1/2 tsp. dried
   oregano
Salt and pepper, to taste

DIRECTIONS

In a large, heavy pot (with a lid), melt the olive oil and butter over medium heat until the butter sizzles. Add the onion, stir for a few minutes, but do not allow it to brown. Add the carrots and celery, and cook for a few more minutes. Add the beef, breaking it up with a fork. Add 1 tsp. of salt and cook gently until the meat is no longer pink, but do not let it brown. Add the wine and turn up the heat, stirring until the wine has nearly evaporated. Add the milk and stir until the milk has evaporated as well. Add the tomatoes, salt, and pepper and bring to a strong simmer. Turn down the heat and allow to cook at a low simmer with the lid partially covering the pot for at least half an hour, stirring occasionally. Taste for salt and add the basil and oregano. Simmer another 10 minutes and taste for seasoning. Serve over pasta with some freshly grated Parmesan cheese, if desired.

SERVES 4–6

During the time when we lived on Tenth Street, my parents bought their first pied-a-terre on Sutton Place in Manhattan. My grandparents lived at the corner of Seventy-Second Street and Central Park West. Although it was very nice to have all that family surrounding us, it was often up to me to help care for my grandparents. We were also obliged to see my parents whenever they were in town, usually once a week. Nana and Papa were not doing well towards the end of their time, and I often brought prepared food to them.

One time, I grabbed whatever I had in my fridge and freezer and brought it uptown to them. One of the items was a frozen mushroom strudel I had made. This is without a doubt, one of my favorite things to make and eat. It was something I often made with my mother in Woodbury and was a great hors d'oeuvre to have ready in the freezer. However, I failed to mark the package (still a problem!). When Papa called to tell me how much they enjoyed the prune pastry, I didn't know whether to laugh or cry.

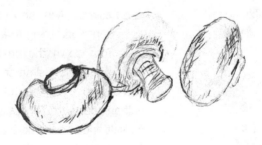

MUSHROOM STRUDEL

INGREDIENTS

2 sticks unsalted butter

4 Tbs. fresh parsley, chopped

2 lbs. mushrooms, finely chopped

2 garlic cloves, minced

1/4 cup dry sherry

Salt and black pepper

4 Tbs. fresh chives, chopped

1 cup sour cream

1 package phyllo dough, defrosted

DIRECTIONS

Sauté the mushrooms with 12 ounces of butter in a large sauté pan over moderate heat. After a few minutes, add the garlic and then the sherry. Stir constantly until the mushrooms have given off their liquid and then the liquid evaporates. Add the parsley, chives, salt and pepper and mix thoroughly. Remove from the heat and add the sour cream. Cover the pan. Melt the rest of the butter and brush one leaf of phyllo with butter, then add a second leaf on top and brush it with butter as well. Place one quarter of the mushroom mixture in a pile along the bottom edge of the phyllo and roll it up and place onto a buttered baking pan. Brush thoroughly with butter. Continue until you have used all the mushroom mixture. Bake for 20 minutes, or until golden, and serve immediately.

SERVES 8–10

Peter and I both began Master's degrees while we lived in Greenwich Village. He started his studies at Pratt Institute in Brooklyn, learning package design on the weekends and evenings. He really enjoyed the program, but after two years he did not earn his Master's in that subject. However, the best part of the annoyance of his having to travel to Brooklyn was that the school was very close to the Arab section of Atlantic Avenue, where we loved to shop and to eat. There was an amazing bakery below the street level that tragically closed about twenty years ago. It was there that I had the very best, never to be duplicated, spinach pies and lamb pies. The taste of them straight out of the ancient ovens was swoon-worthy. My mouth is literally watering as I type this! Here is the approximation of what truly can never be as good, but is good enough! As they say, don't let perfect get in the way of great—or something like that.

SPINACH AND/OR LAMB PIES

INGREDIENTS

Pita Dough
1 package dry yeast (1 Tbs.)
1 1/2 cups warm water
1/2 tsp. honey
1 Tbs. olive oil plus more for
   brushing the pies
1 tsp. kosher salt
3 ½ cuop all-purpose flour

DIRECTIONS

Combine the yeast with the water and honey and mix thoroughly. Allow to rest for 5 minutes to test the freshness of the yeast. The mixture should have begun to foam if the yeast is working. If not, throw it out and start again with new yeast. Add the flour, oil, and salt. Turn out on to a floured surface and knead for 10 minutes and then cover with plastic wrap and allow to rise for an hour. Divide into 12 pieces and roll into balls. Cover and let rest for 5 minutes.

Spinach and/or Lamb Filling
3 Tbs. olive oil
1 bunch scallions
3 cups spinach or 1 lb. ground
   lamb
1/4 cup pine nuts
1/2 tsp. allspice
1 tsp. dried sumac, optional
1 tsp. za'atar, optional
Juice of 1 lemon
Semolina for the pan

In a large sauté pan, heat the olive oil and add the scallions. Sauté about 5 minutes and add the spinach or lamb, pine nuts, and seasonings. Continue to cook until the spinach has wilted or the lamb is no longer pink. Add the lemon juice and mix thoroughly. Preheat the oven to 350°. Roll out the dough balls on a floured surface into 6-inch circles. Brush the circles with olive oil and then place 2 Tbs. of the filling into the center of each. Pinch 3 corners together, covering the filling completely. Brush with oil, bake on a baking sheet sprinkled with semolina, and bake for 15 minutes or until golden.

At any time in my life, I had no idea at all what I wanted to be when I grew up. It sounds bizarre, but I had no dreams, no passions, except for cooking. I told my dad that I wanted to go to the newly opened Culinary Institute of America to become a professional, either to be a chef or to write for a food magazine, like *Gourmet*. He literally scoffed at the idea and said that I would "get fat" if I became a chef and that he would not pay for it. End of story! And sadly, he was such a powerful influence that I did not pursue it!

Instead, I spoke with a college friend who was getting a master's in Community Organization Social Work at Yeshiva University. He told me that it was very common for the graduates of the program to move to Israel ("making aliyah") and find good jobs there. This appealed to me in a very deep way. I had often thought that Peter and I would move to Israel, and this seemed like a good way to have a foot in the door when we got there. We even took Hebrew *Ulpan* (Intensive) lessons together, which instantly gave Peter an ulcer.

My first field work assignment in graduate school was in Bensonhurst, Brooklyn, where I soon became part of the Bensonhurst Mental Health Players. We did drama therapy by performing at community organizations, such as churches and mental health clinics, around the themes of family and community issues. I really loved doing this work, but it was only a small part of my duties. The rest of the time I was asked to observe children at risk in Catholic schools in the area and to assist at board meetings for the Mental Health Clinic.

My second year at Yeshiva U. had me going to New Jersey on the PATH train from Greenwich Village to East Orange to work at the Jewish Federation. I was assigned to work with the Young Singles group and the Psychologist group to help them organize meetings to raise funds for various community needs. One interesting project I had with the psychologists group was to organize a rally on behalf of Soviet Jewry. This was the time when the first Jews in Soviet Russia were given permission to leave, and we had about two hundred people attend the rally.

The Young Singles group was comprised mostly of what I would call "nerds in glasses with pocket protectors" looking to find their special someone in this group. I was at least ten years younger than most of them, married—and what was worse, I was obviously pregnant. They were not very interested in what I had to offer, to say the least. Riding the PATH train, and then the bus, and then walking a few blocks in rough East Orange became a real chore, especially as summer approached and at seven months pregnant. They offered me a job at the end of my training, but I turned them down; I was not at all interested in working for the Federation.

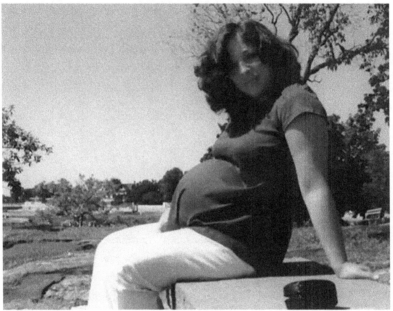
August 1982

I spent the summer getting ready to take the certification exam, which was six hours long and scheduled one week before my due date in September. We lived near some very good restaurants, bakeries, and food stores, which I frequented now that I had time. My craving was very often for the amazing light and fluffy matzo balls in chicken soup from the Second Avenue Deli, which was only a few blocks from us.

CHICKEN SOUP WITH MATZO BALLS

INGREDIENTS

5 lbs. chicken pieces, preferably thighs, wings, necks, backs (skinned)
1 Tbs. kosher salt
4–5 quarts water
1 onion, cut in half, skin on
2 carrots, peeled and left whole
4 celery stalks with tops
1 parsnip, cut in half
1 turnip, cut in half
1 bunch parsley
1 bunch dill
1 clove garlic, cut in half

Frozen Matzo Balls

2 eggs, beaten
2 Tbs. chicken fat or oil
1/2 tsp. sea salt
Dash of black pepper
1/2 cup matzo meal
1/4 cup seltzer
1 Tbs. fresh dill or parsley, chopped fine
Can of nonstick spray (like Pam)
1 plastic ice-cube tray

DIRECTIONS

Wash the chicken thoroughly and place in a soup pot with the salt and cold water. Bring to a boil, removing scum as it appears, then turn down heat and partially cover, and simmer for half an hour. Add the rest of the ingredients and simmer partially covered for another hour. Taste for seasoning, remove everything (keep the carrot and slice thinly) and strain before adding the matzo balls!

In a medium bowl, combine the eggs, fat, salt, and pepper. Add the matzo meal and then slowly add the seltzer. Stir until combined. Refrigerate for half an hour. Spray the ice-cube tray with the nonstick spray. Pour the mixture into the trays, filling to the top of each compartment. Freeze until ready to cook in a large covered pot in salted water for half an hour, trying not to peek! Add to soup after they have cooked thoroughly.

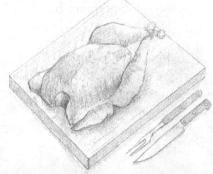

The baby was over a week late and I was going crazy waiting, so we took a friend's advice and walked over a mile to Sammy's Roumanian restaurant and ate a lot of very garlicky, fatty, delicious Jewish food and walked the very long walk back home. A few hours later, as hoped, I went into labor. Thirty-two hours and very many contractions later, I had a Cesarean section, and Adam was born.

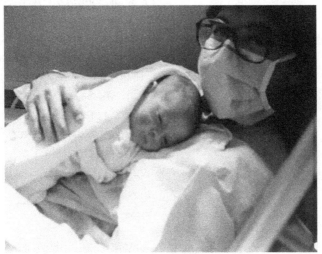

Adam, one hour after birth

It was our tradition for many years to go back to Sammy's for Adam's birthday. Sammy's is sadly shuttered now, but Adam often went there with his friends for his birthday (parents were not invited!). It was a subterranean dive with an entertainer and was designed to make you feel as though you were a guest at a Bar Mitzvah. There was a *schmaltz* (chicken fat) dispenser on the table, fantastic pickled peppers, and every kind of Jewish food you have heard of—and many that you probably have not (unborn eggs)! It was a party every time you went and there were many dishes you cannot find at any other restaurant, such as stuffed derma, chopped liver with *gribenes*, and *karnatzlach*. Gribenes are the little bits of crunchy chicken skin and onions that are cooked in schmaltz and are devilishly delicious. They are astoundingly yummy on mashed potatoes but are a wonderful treat on their own.

GRIBENES WITH ONION

INGREDIENTS

Chicken skin

Onions (half the amount of skin)

Salt and black pepper

DIRECTIONS

Cut the skin into small pieces and put it in a small sauté pan over low heat. When it has begun to crisp, which could take almost an hour, add the chopped onions, salt, and pepper and cook until the onions brown and the skin is brown. Serve with chopped liver, mashed potatoes or out of hand. (There never seems to be any left for chopped liver or mashed potatoes in our house).

I was not very happy living in New York City with a baby because getting anywhere with a baby carriage was a logistical nightmare. Forget about using the subway, the bus, or even a taxi with a carriage; it was just impossible. Luckily there were a number of excellent places in our immediate area to visit with the stroller. Tuesday was the day to visit the "Egg Lady" on Twelfth Street, Balducci's was only a few blocks away for excellent meat, Murray's Cheese was within walking distance, the Union Square Market on Saturday was very close by for farm-fresh produce, and Moishe's Bakery on Second Avenue sold the very best chocolate *babka* ever. We recently drove by it and sadly saw that it had finally closed its doors.

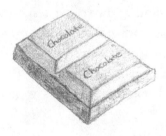

CHOCOLATE BABKA

INGREDIENTS

4–5 cups all-purpose flour
1/2 cup super-fine sugar
1 Tbs. fast-acting yeast
3 eggs
1/2 cup whole milk
1/4 tsp. sea salt
2/3 cup softened unsalted
   butter, cut into small pieces

Filling

1/2 cup powdered sugar
1/3 cup best-quality cocoa
   powder
4 oz. semisweet chocolate
   chips, melted with 1/2 cup
   unsalted butter
1 cup pecans, chopped
2 Tbs. superfine sugar

DIRECTIONS

In a standing mixer, combine 4 cups of flour, sugar, and yeast. Add the eggs, milk, and salt—and mix well. Add the butter a little at a time until the dough has formed, adding a little flour if needed to bring the dough together, and continue mixing for 10 minutes or until shiny and smooth. Remove and place in a plastic bag and refrigerate for several hours or overnight. Grease the bottom and sides of two loaf pans and line the bottom with parchment paper. In a small bowl, combine the powdered sugar, cocoa, melted chocolate, and butter. Divide the dough in half. Roll one half out on a lightly floured surface to form a 10 x 14 rectangle. Spread half the filling over the surface and sprinkle with half the pecans and half the superfine sugar, and roll tightly from the long side, pressing to seal at the ends. Place the roll on its seam, and using a long sharp knife, cut it in half lengthwise. With the cut sides facing up, gently lay the two slices side-by-side and braid by lifting right side over left and left side over right. Press both ends together and place into the loaf pan. Repeat with the other piece of dough. Cover with damp tea towels and place in a warm place to rise for about an hour.

Preheat the oven to 375°. Remove the towels, sprinkle with the remaining sugar, and bake in the center of the oven for about 45 minutes or until golden and a wooden skewer comes out clean when inserted into the middle of the cake. Let cakes remain in the pan for about 10 minutes and then turn out onto racks to cool.

YIELD: 2 LOAF CAKES

Our apartment had only one bedroom, so we transformed the dining room into a temporary nursery for Adam. Unfortunately, he was (and still is) a very light sleeper, and the dining room was right off the kitchen, so every time I tried to cook while he slept the slightest noise awakened him with a *geshrei* (scream). We decided to leave Manhattan, and despite our misgivings about living near Peter's parents, we bought a sweet house in Larchmont and moved there on January 19, 1983.

Waving goodbye to 70 East Tenth Street

CHAPTER 7

45 ISELIN TERRACE
LARCHMONT, NEW YORK
JANUARY 1983-JUNE 1994

We moved into our new house in Westchester County, New York, on the nineteenth of January and awoke the next morning to a huge snowstorm. It was very beautiful, but the last thing we thought to bring from the city was a snow shovel, and the roads were all closed. I hesitantly rang the doorbell at the house across the street to ask to borrow a shovel. I was greeted by a boy of ten and his sister, a couple of years younger than he, and their mother, Lynn. They were very excited to have new neighbors with a baby. It was our first encounter with the very best thing about living in the suburbs—neighbors!

It was only a matter of days, or perhaps a week, that we met all of our many neighbors. Our deep backyard was in the center of the block and surrounded by eight other backyards. We found babysitters diagonally across the street, friends next door, and eventually, friends for all our future children within a block or two. It was a dream that we could simply walk outside and immediately encounter friends.

Peter left for work the day after the snowstorm, driving back and forth from New Jersey, often with his father, who lived about a mile or so from us. I was home with the new baby, cleaning the mess the previous owners had left behind and trying to unpack

Adam and me (second day in our new house)

our things while caring for Adam at the same time. Eventually, I was worn out and got a very bad case of the flu. I was literally lying on the floor when Peter's mom, Pat, walked in unannounced. I was too sick to be embarrassed and tried to get up when I noticed that she had brought with her homemade chicken in the pot. This was her very sweet way to help me get through the flu. I was touched beyond words.

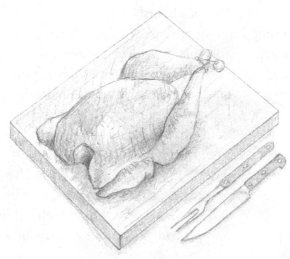

CHICKEN IN THE POT WITH MATZO BALLS

INGREDIENTS

1 4-lb. kosher chicken (preferably a pullet), cut in 8 pieces

1 veal knuckle, optional but flavorful

1–2 tsp. chicken fat or oil

1 qt. good-quality chicken stock

1/2 cup white wine

3/4 cup pearl onions, peeled— or 1 yellow onion, chopped

1 leek, halved and cut in 1-inch pieces

2 celery stalks, cut in 1-inch pieces

2 carrots, peeled and cut in 1-inch pieces

2 parsnips, peeled and cut in 1-inch pieces

3 garlic cloves, peeled and cut in half

1 sprig fresh dill and 1 bay leaf

5 peppercorns

1 clove

1 tsp. salt, or to taste

4 cups water

Matzo Balls (see recipe)

6 oz. *fedelini* (or very fine egg noodles), cooked

1/2 cup shelled or frozen peas (do not defrost)

DIRECTIONS

Preheat the oven to 375°. Wash and skin the chicken. (You may save the skin for *gribenes*. See recipe). Heat the fat or oil over medium heat on the stove in an oven-proof casserole with a lid. Pat the chicken dry, and when the oil is hot, brown the chicken and the veal knuckle on all sides. Remove the chicken and the veal bone from the pan and deglaze the pan with the wine, stirring until all the brown bits have been loosened. Add the stock and return the chicken and the veal bone to the pot. Add all the vegetables, the seasonings, and the water. Bring to a boil, cover, and carefully place in the oven for an hour and a half. Check the pot to see that it is simmering continuously.

While the chicken is in the oven, begin the matzo balls. After preparing the batter, pour the mixture into the greased ice cube tray and freeze for 1 hour. Bring a pot of salted water to a boil and carefully "pop" the matzo balls into the pot. Bring to a boil, turn down the heat, and simmer (covered) for half an hour. Carefully remove the casserole from the oven. Discard the veal bone. (The dish can be prepared ahead until this point and refrigerated.) Add the cooked matzo balls, the noodles, and the peas—and simmer over medium heat for 10 minutes. Remove the veal bone and any other bones that are easily removed.

SERVES 4–6 AS A MAIN DISH

A few weeks later, I was still unpacking when I saw a mom pushing a stroller passed the house. I literally ran out of the door and introduced myself and told her I had a baby the same size. We quickly became friends, and the boys played together for the next few years. Roberta introduced me to the only soup that her son, Michael, would eat. Adam loved it, and everything else I ever gave him to eat. Roberta's Beef Barley Soup remains to this day, a favorite of infant and parent alike.

ROBERTA'S BEEF BARLEY SOUP

INGREDIENTS

1/2 lb. beef flanken or stew
1 Tbs. olive oil
1 large onion, chopped
2 stalks celery, sliced
2 carrots, peeled and chopped
2 cloves garlic, thinly sliced
1 Tbs. butter
1 Tbs. flour
2 quarts vegetable/chicken
broth, warmed
1 cup whole pearl barley
1 bay leaf
1 tsp. dried, or 2 tsp. fresh,
thyme
Salt and pepper to taste

DIRECTIONS

In a soup pot, sauté the beef in the oil until browned on both sides, then add the onion, celery, carrot, and garlic—and cook over medium heat. After the vegetables have softened, add the butter and flour, and stir thoroughly. Add the broth and bring to a boil over high heat. Add the barley, bay leaf, thyme, salt, and pepper—and turn the heat to low. Partially cover and simmer for about half an hour or until the barley is cooked. Taste for seasoning.

SERVES 4

By the time we had finished unpacking we realized that the kitchen was sorely in need of a makeover. We hired a construction crew whom we knew from our apartment building to come to Westchester to create a new kitchen. They were originally from Puerto Rico, and when they finished the work, we invited them to dinner at the house. I had the chutzpah to make a Puerto Rican dinner, which I hoped would bring back good memories. I made *arroz con pollo* with plantains for dinner and a caramel flan for dessert.

CARAMEL FLAN

INGREDIENTS

2/3 cup plus 1/3 cup superfine white sugar
2 Tbs. water
1 1/2 cups heavy cream
1 1/2 cups whole milk
1/4 tsp. salt
6 egg yolks
1 Tbs. vanilla extract

DIRECTIONS

Preheat the oven to 350°. Place a glass pie pan or 6 custard cups near the stove. Melt the 2/3 cup of sugar and the water over medium heat in a small saucepan, stirring only until the crystals have dissolved, then heating until deeply brown, twirling the pan every so often, being very careful not to burn it. Quickly pour the syrup evenly into the pie pan or cups, tilting to cover the bottom with the caramel. Heat the cream and milk in a heavy saucepan over medium-high heat until bubbles appear around the edges of the pan. Immediately add the remaining sugar, stirring until dissolved. Place the egg yolks into a large bowl and whisk well. Mix in the extract and then add the cream and milk mixture. Strain the mixture and pour into the pan.

Place about 1 inch of boiling water into a large baking pan and put it into the center of the preheated oven. Carefully place the custard pan or cups into the baking pan and bake for 30 minutes for the pan, or 20 minutes for the cups, or until the custard has set (when a knife inserted in the center comes out clean). Cool on a rack, then cover with plastic wrap and refrigerate until well-chilled. Run a knife around the edge of the pan and turn over onto a serving dish.

SERVES 6-8

Our neighbors across the street soon introduced us to their cousins who lived around the corner, Dan and Vicki, and their two-year-old son, Alex. A few days after meeting them I was with Adam at Roberta and Michael's when their neighbors from across the street (Vicki and Alex) dropped by. It was immediately clear that Alex was no ordinary two-year-old, as he put together a twenty-five-piece puzzle in a matter of minutes. Vicki asked me whether we belonged to a synagogue, and I told her that we had unhappily joined the Larchmont Temple because Peter's parents were founding members, but that it was too formal and grey-haired for us. She told me about the *Chavurah* (small group of Jews who pray outside of the institutional setting) that they were a part of, and that changed our lives forever.

When I was a Jewish Studies major at Connecticut College, I wrote my Senior Thesis on *Chavurot* (plural of Chavurah), so it was extremely exciting for me to actually go to services at one in the immediate area. Services at Chavurah Tikvah are held in one of the twenty-five-family members' homes and are created by the members, accompanied by songs on a guitar. The instant we sat down at one of the services, we knew this was where we needed to worship and raise our children. The group was very central to our lives for the next twenty years and was the focus of our spiritual and social experience. Every Jewish holiday was spent with this group—and these were authentic and mostly joyous times. The people were creative, smart, and dedicated—and we were instantly enriched with a unique and rewarding community experience.

Hanukkah was festive and fun and always included Vicki's table where she helped the kids make *sufganiyot* (Hanukkah donuts), right there at the party. Dipping the hot donuts into blue sugar before serving them was Adam's favorite activity. I was always nervous about the children working with the hot oil, but thankfully there were no catastrophes.

SUFGANIYOT—
ISRAELI HANUKKAH DONUTS

INGREDIENTS

1 1/2 cups white flour

1 1/2 cups buttermilk

1 Tbs. white sugar

1 1/2 tsp. baking powder

1 egg, beaten

1 tsp. vanilla extract

2 cups vegetable oil

1/2 cup raspberry or apricot
jam

1/2 cup white sugar

DIRECTIONS

Heat the oil in a wok or frying pan to 375° (on a candy thermometer). In a medium bowl combine the flour, buttermilk, 1 Tbs. sugar, egg, and vanilla. Drop the batter by tablespoons into the oil, frying 3 or 4 at a time until brown on the bottom. Turn over the donuts with a pair of tongs and brown on the other side. Drain the donuts on paper towels. Heat the jam in the microwave for 45 seconds in order to thin it. Use a small knife to cut a slit halfway through each donut. Take a turkey baster and squirt about 1 tsp. of jam into the hole in the donut. Roll the donuts in the sugar and serve immediately.

SERVES 4

When Adam was about a year old, I received a call from one of my professors at Yeshiva University asking if I would come to work as a Development Associate for the Social Work Graduate School. It was really a perfect way to re-enter the work force as it was one-day-a-week in a university setting with people I admired, so I quickly agreed. Yeshiva University is located in Washington Heights (in the very north of Manhattan), and we lived only half an hour away in Westchester. I could do that! The tricky part was finding a babysitter for Adam.

I tentatively asked my mother if she would drive up from Long Island on Tuesdays so that I could take the job. She agreed to come as long as she could leave by 3:00 p.m. to avoid driving at rush hour and in the dark. I hired a young girl from the high school to come in the afternoons. I enjoyed the work, which was mostly trying to get alumni to give donations to the school by creating group programming in various locations. In addition, I was asked to do book reviews for the *Jewish Social Work Journal*. It was very exciting to see my writing published.

However, the very favorite part of my day at work was lunch (no big surprise there!). The university had an automat in the cafeteria that specialized in kosher specialties that I could not get in Larchmont. My favorite was a vegetarian chopped liver sandwich, which does not sound nearly as yummy as it was.

VEGETARIAN CHOPPED LIVER

INGREDIENTS

1 medium onion, chopped
1 Tbs. vegetable oil
1/2 tsp. black pepper
1 tsp. kosher salt
1/2 cup canned mushrooms, drained
3/4 cup frozen green beans, defrosted
3/4 cup walnuts
2 hard-boiled eggs
Freshly ground black pepper

DIRECTIONS

Heat a frying pan and then add the chopped onion. Sprinkle the onion with the black pepper. Cook for about 5 minutes or until the onion has turned opaque and is "jumping" in the pan. Add the oil and the salt and fry until the onions are light brown. Place the mushrooms, green beans, walnuts, and eggs in a wooden chopping bowl or into a food processor. Chop until fine and then add the onions. Chill and then taste for seasoning.

SERVES 4

I spent the rest of the week like most suburban stay-at-home moms, driving to Mommy and Me classes, Gymboree, the play-ground—and in the summer, to the town beach. We were very lucky to have Manor Beach on the Long Island Sound only a bike ride away. I would strap Adam into the baby seat on the back of my bike and go the mile or so to the beach, where we had a locker to hold all the necessities. There was a grill that served burgers and a few other items, but mostly, I packed the food we needed for the day. Adam was a very good eater and enjoyed just about everything he tasted. I usually packed leftovers from the evening before, and we would sit up at the picnic tables and feast on cold lamb chops and corn on the cob.

One day I was trying to shlep all of Adam's toys, chairs, towels, and who knows what else down the stairs to the beach when a pair of arms came out of nowhere to help me. I glanced up at this angelic woman in a gold bathing suit, with long wavy blond hair and an obviously pregnant belly. Her young son, Ben, who turned out to be exactly Adam's age, was waiting at the bottom of the stairs. We spent the day together at the beach, and Lauren and I became very close friends for many years to come.

That autumn, Lauren and Ben came over to visit, and I had made some of my mother's delicious miniature potato *knishes*. They are so yummy because the onions are sautéed in chicken fat (shmaltz), which infuses the potatoes, making them savory and rich. So rich, that Ben, who had eaten about ten of them, promptly threw up. It was embarrassing for her and for me as well, as I felt badly for having served it to them in the first place.

MINI POTATO KNISHES

INGREDIENTS

1 package prepared pie crust (the roll-out version), thawed
2 lbs. potatoes, peeled and cubed
1 large onion, diced
1 Tbs. melted chicken or duck fat or olive oil
Chicken stock or water
1 egg, lightly beaten with 1 Tbs. water
Salt and black pepper

DIRECTIONS

Set oven to 375°. Boil the potatoes in water to cover until soft when poked with a sharp knife. Mash with a potato masher. While the potatoes are cooking, heat the fat or oil on medium heat in a saucepan. When hot, add the onions and sauté until lightly browned, about 10 minutes or so. Add the browned onions to the mashed potatoes and some stock or water if it is very thick, and add salt and pepper to taste. Roll out the pie crust onto a lightly floured surface and, using a rolling pin, thin out the crust evenly. Using a drinking glass, cut out circles in the dough and keep cutting and rerolling until all the pie crust has been used. Add about a teaspoon of the potatoes to the center of the circles and form triangles by pinching three corners towards the center. Place the knishes onto ungreased cookie sheets, which can be placed close to one another, as they do not expand. After all the knishes have been put onto cookie sheets, brush the egg mixture over the surface of them. Bake for about 10 minutes or until golden brown.

SERVES 4

Lauren was due very soon with her second child, whom she named Julie. Not long after Julie was born, I learned that we were to have our second child, and Lauren suggested that if it were a girl, Lauren would be a great name—but that turned out not to be appropriate.

Starting with my work at Yeshiva University, my mother would come to babysit every Tuesday. I finished my job at YU in early June of 1985, and the baby was due a few weeks later, but my mom kept up her Tuesday visits. On Tuesday, June 18, Mom came as usual, and we had a lovely day. When it was time for her to drive back to Long Island, I noticed that I was having contractions. She suggested that she stay because I had asked her to be with Adam when we were in the hospital. However, I was convinced that it was false labor, called Braxton-Hicks contractions, and sent her home.

However, a few hours later it was clear that, in fact, they were true contractions. I called my parents and asked them to come as we were going to be leaving for the hospital. My father said that he had to see patients in the morning and would not come. I was furious and hung up on him. My mother called back and said that despite the fact that it was raining and would mean driving over the bridge in the dark, she would come alone! That woman could always be counted on when it really mattered. I don't think I was ever more grateful or proud of her. You can just imagine how I felt about my dad!

I had been in labor with Adam for thirty-two hours and it had ended with a Cesarean section. I was determined not to repeat that torturous scenario, so I chose a doctor who was successful in natural births following Cesareans, which were called VBACs. We arrived at the hospital after about eight hours of labor, only to discover that the doctor was away on vacation. After seven more hours, it was decided that I would need to have another Cesarean, and very shortly thereafter, the operating room nurse announced that we had a beautiful red-headed boy!

Peter and I are both brunettes, so it was shocking to hear that we had a redhead; I even looked around the room to see if there was another family having a baby! We had decided that if we had a boy, he would be named Jeremy. After a day or two in the hospital, we came to the conclusion that this was no Jeremy, which seemed to be the name for a calm and gentle child. This little guy was already very active and full of life, so we named him Zachary Ethan, which suited his personality much better.

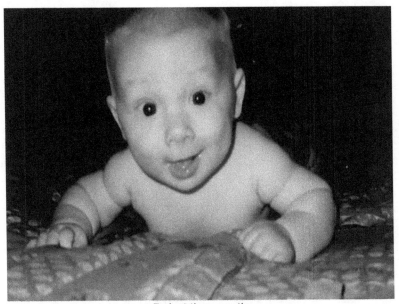

Zach at three months

It was very lovely living on Iselin Terrace in those days, as there were many families with young children surrounding us. When I was pregnant with Zach, I met a young woman named Nancy, also due with her second child, who lived right up the street and had a son who was Adam's age. Nancy's son, Ryan, and Adam had a tenuous relationship, but Nancy and I really enjoyed being together, so we tried to get the two of them to get along. Right before Zach was born, Nancy had Sean, and then we saw each other a great deal more.

Zach and Sean were inseparable from the moment that they could crawl. Nancy had grown up on Staten Island in an Irish family and had married Craig, who had grown up in Pennsylvania in a large and quite famous family who practiced the Swedenborg religion. They were so different from anyone we had been friends with before, and it was very refreshing. We spent many days together and they invited us to Craig's parent's mountain camp in the Poconos. We later invited them to Peter's parent's house on Sanibel Island, Florida.

They invited us for Christmas dinner and we invited them for our holiday meals. I had never been a guest for Christmas, and it was quite an honor, although looking back on it, the guests were just us, so it wasn't that big a deal. But at the time it was all very new and very special. Nancy was a pragmatic cook, who prepared what needed to be made, but everything was always tasty and child-friendly. One of the best dishes I tasted of hers were her Christmas pecan cookies. Everyone who tastes them loves them—and no one ever guesses the secret, which is that they are based on whole graham crackers.

NANCY'S PECAN COOKIES

INGREDIENTS

1 1/2 cellophane packages
   graham crackers
2 sticks unsalted butter
1/2 cup white sugar
1 cup chopped pecans

DIRECTIONS

Preheat the oven to 350°. Line a shallow cookie sheet with aluminum foil. Separate the graham crackers into individual pieces and line edge-to-edge on the cookie sheet. In a large glass measuring cup, melt the butter in the microwave for about 45 seconds. Stir in the sugar and microwave on high for 2 minutes. Stir in the pecan pieces and pour evenly over the graham crackers. Bake for 17 minutes. Allow to cool and then break into cookies.

One day I served them noodle *kugel*, which was one of Zach's favorite dishes. He had quite a sweet tooth and preferred beige food to anything else. Not so today! He has been an extremely healthy eater since high school and would never eat it now.

NOODLE PUDDING-LOKSHEN KUGEL

INGREDIENTS

1 lb. egg noodles, cooked al
   dente
1 stick butter, melted
6 eggs, beaten
1 cup honey
16 oz. small-curd cottage
   cheese
16 oz. sour cream
2 cups sweetened corn flakes
Cinnamon
Pinch of salt
1/2 stick butter for topping,
   melted

DIRECTIONS

Preheat oven to 350°. In a large bowl, combine everything except the last four ingredients. Grease a 9 x 12-inch baking dish. Empty bowl into greased 9 x 12-inch pan. Combine the last four ingredients and sprinkle onto the noodles. Bake for 1 hour or until cooked throughout: Insert a table knife in center; pudding is done if the knife is dry when removed; if it emerges coated with mixture, bake for 10 more minutes and try again. (Can be frozen.)
SERVES 8

Nancy was friendly with a woman around the block named Diana, who had a son Sean's and Zach's age. Diana was married to a man from Australia, and when Zach was about eight years old, they introduced him to Australian culture: the music, the stories, and the food. He was fascinated by the music of the didgeridoo, and eventually we bought him one. He begged for a boomerang, and we regretfully bought him one of those, as well. We allowed him to use it only in wide open spaces, which were hard to come by in Westchester, and there were some very near misses. He came home requesting that I make him everything he tasted at their house. We ate meat pies with mushy peas (yuck) and fairy bread (yum). Diana gave me the recipe for the most delicious shortbread I had ever tasted; ginger shortbread.

GINGER SHORTBREAD

INGREDIENTS

6 Tbs. butter, melted

1 egg, beaten

1 cup sugar

1/4 tsp. salt

1 3/4 cups all-purpose flour, plus more as needed

1/2 cup crystallized ginger, cut into 1/4-cubes

Almonds, for decoration

DIRECTIONS

Heat oven to 325°. Line an 8-inch round cake pan with parchment paper and grease the sides and bottom with butter. Remove one teaspoon of beaten egg and set aside. Place the melted butter in a small bowl and add the rest of the egg. In a medium bowl combine the sugar, salt, and flour. Add the butter and egg mixture. Mix in the ginger. Press into the cake pan. Brush with the egg. Decorate the top with the almonds. Using a sharp knife, score the surface about 1/2-inch deep, with 4 lines from end to end creating 8 triangles. Bake for 40 minutes or until just golden. Allow to cool before serving.

SERVES 8

When Zach was about two years old, I decided that we could use some live-in help, because the two boys demanded so much of my attention, and the house badly needed some focus too. We were considering having a third child, and I wanted a housecleaner, not a babysitter, so I hired a woman from Guyana whose name was Rampati. She was very good at cleaning but also at sensing when it was family time and disappearing—only to reappear when it was time to clean up.

She came from a very simple background, so a lot of modern technology was completely out of her realm of experience—such as sheets, light bulbs, telephones. These were all new to her, and she had to be instructed how to use them. Today, I cannot believe I could leave the house with someone watching my children who could not use the phone.

Rampati with Doris (Pat's housekeeper)

However, she was very loving and a great help to me. She and Adam got along very well (I have never met anyone who doesn't get along with Adam), but Zach was not happy to have her take care of him. Rampati's parents were brought to Guyana from India, so she prepared many dishes from her heritage, including a lentil-stuffed bread called *roti*, which we all loved. She taught me to make the very best, most delicious *dal* ever. Dal usually tastes like library paste—not that I have ever eaten library paste! This version has very deep flavors and a distinct tang from lemon juice and rind. The only caveat I have is that you will never enjoy restaurant dal again!

LEMON LENTIL DAL

INGREDIENTS

1/2 cup vegetable oil or ghee (clarified butter)

1 large onion, halved and thinly sliced

1 cinnamon stick

2 cups dry, split, red lentils

2 tsp. fresh ginger, grated

3 cups vegetable broth

2 cups water

1/2 tsp. cayenne powder, or to taste

1 lemon, squeezed (reserve the skin)

1/2 cup chopped shallots

1 garlic clove, minced

1/2 hot green chili, chopped (seeds and ribs removed)

2 bay leaves

1/2 cup fresh cilantro leaves, chopped

Kosher salt, to taste

DIRECTIONS

In a large saucepan, sauté the onion slices in 1/4 cup of oil or ghee over medium heat until they are transparent. Add the cinnamon sticks, lentils, and the ginger—and cook for about 10 minutes. Add the broth and the water, along with about 1 tsp. of salt and the cayenne—and bring to a boil. Turn down the heat to medium, add the lemon juice and the lemon—and cook for about 45 minutes, stirring often. In a small frying pan, heat the rest of the oil or ghee over medium heat and add the shallots, garlic, chili, and bay leaves. Cook until the shallots have browned. Add this to the cooked lentils, stir well, and sprinkle with the cilantro.

SERVES 4–6

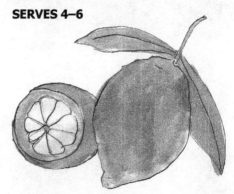

Rampati used to "mash" the boys' legs; which was a massage to help them relax before bed. We sponsored her so as to allow her to stay in the US with her children, who lived in Queens, which meant that she had to live with us for the next three years. During this time, we decided to have another child, so having her at home made it possible for me to care for my kids without having to worry about the housework.

I found a new obstetrician who agreed with me that trying for natural childbirth was too risky, so we set the date for the Cesarean for April 1. However, my mother objected and said that no grandchild of hers was going to be born on April Fool's Day, and so we changed the date to March 31st.

From the moment we brought this beautiful boy, Tobias Samuel, home, he and Rampati were very close. Eventually he called her "Pati," and he was always very happy to have her babysit when I needed to leave the house.

Right before Toby was born, my grandparents, Nana and Papa, passed away one right after the other—and as is Jewish custom, we incorporated their names in his. Toby's middle name, Samuel is a

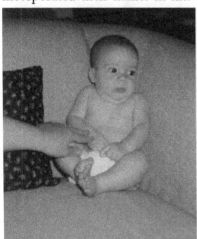

combination of Sara and Maury. They left me a very generous amount in their will, considering that they lived like church-mice all their years. They always rented their apartments and counted their pennies. I was so touched by their thoughtfulness that we decided to buy a small weekend house in the country with the money they left me.

Tobias Samuel, three months old

CHAPTER 8

214 DAWSON ROAD
HILLSDALE, NEW YORK
JANUARY 1988

We were very uncertain as to where we wanted to own a second home, but we knew that our family needed more nature, more privacy, and a place where we had some time to be together as a family without the distractions of work, friends, and obligations. When I was eight-months pregnant with Toby, Peter found an ad in the *New York Times* about a small home in upstate New York, built as a schoolhouse in the 1860s, filled with "antiques," on three acres. The house was in Hillsdale, Columbia County, which borders the northern Hudson Valley and the Berkshire Mountains of western Massachusetts.

We had visited my cousin, Nina, in the area the year before and we loved the combination of nature and culture, with both skiing and Tanglewood so close by. It was only a two-hour drive from Westchester and was offered at a price we could afford. Peter went up to see it—as I was not up for a four-hour drive in one day—and fell in love. He tried to put a deposit down on the house at that moment, but the realtor said she would not let him do that until I saw it as well. It was late January, with about three feet of snow covering the grounds and the thermometer stuck at a piercing 10 degrees, but we bundled up Adam and Zach and traveled up to Hillsdale.

One look at the enormous screened porch was all that I needed to agree that it was a perfect second home for us. The next chapter is devoted to the country house, but we lived on Iselin Terrace for six more years before moving to another home in Larchmont. Those six years were not the easiest of times for our family. Peter's business was having trouble keeping up with the factories in China and his parents became very ill and needed his attention, Adam was struggling in school, and Zach and Toby were constantly at each other. All in all, our escape to Hillsdale whenever possible was the antidote to most of our troubles. However necessary it was to get away, we were inevitably forced to return to reality on Iselin Terrace.

At the end of January, we closed on the house and kept most of the "antique" furniture that came with it. The furniture was definitely old, but not necessarily antique, and we had neither the time nor the funds to buy all new furniture. It was fine for weekends and okay for the summer. The purpose of this place was not the drab indoors but the exquisite outdoors. Peter took the kids to nearby Catamount for skiing, which they (not I) all eagerly enjoyed. At the house, we went cross-country skiing, made snowmen, went sledding down the enormous hill across the street, skated in nearby ponds, and made maple taffy in the snow. When we were inside, we played games, watched movies, and really enjoyed our solitude, which was an impossibility in Larchmont.

Although the house had four bedrooms, we slept only in the two that were downstairs—we in one, and the three boys in the other. The upstairs was used for guests. It was very cozy, and we felt like we were roughing it in the woods. We often had weekend guests, which was a strain on the plumbing and the kitchen, but it offered some distraction from the intensity of the cabin experience.

The kitchen was a very tight galley design that had a very small amount of counter space and orange Formica on the counters. The only window in the area was over the washing machine, adjacent to the kitchen, which I could barely see out of. There was absolutely no aesthetic to the space, but it was functional, and that was all that was needed when you have three small boys.

During the first summer we owned the house in the country,

I decided that Adam would briefly go to the local day camp in Westchester. And then we would spend the rest of the summer in Hillsdale, being in nature and on our own. Peter left Monday morning to work in New Jersey at the family factory and returned Thursday evening. That left me with the boys all week. Dinner was often whatever the little guys would eat—chicken nuggets, spaghetti, hamburgers, etc.

However, Adam ate everything I liked to eat, so I would make something a bit more interesting for the two of us to go along with the kiddie food. I have always loved gardening, and now with three acres of land I was free to have as large a garden as I could manage. We were often overloaded with zucchini, tomatoes, and beans.

I don't think I owned a credit card in those days, so Peter would give me what we thought would be enough cash to last me until he returned. I often ran out of cash by Wednesday, so dinner would be whatever was in the fridge or in the garden. Adam and I ate an awful lot of zucchini one August. This recipe was a favorite, as I grew a lot of basil and there was an egg distribution plant literally right up the road from us.

ZUCCHINI BASIL FRITTATAS

INGREDIENTS

1 lb. small zucchini, grated
Kosher salt
4 Tbs. olive oil
3 garlic cloves, minced
6 eggs
1/4 cup grated Parmesan
1/4 cup finely shredded fresh
  basil
Black pepper to taste

DIRECTIONS

Place the zucchini shreds in a colander and sprinkle with the salt. Allow to drain for 30 minutes and then press out the liquid. Heat half the olive oil in a small skillet and sauté the garlic. Add the zucchini and cook over high heat until the moisture evaporates and the zucchini turns bright green. Preheat the broiler. Beat the eggs in a medium bowl and add the Parmesan cheese, basil, and black pepper. Heat the remaining olive oil in a large oven-proof pan over medium heat, add the egg mixture and lower the heat, allowing the bottom to cook. When only the top remains uncooked, place the frittata under the broiler to finish cooking. Flip onto a serving plate and serve at room temperature.

SERVES 4

During the first summer we stayed in the country, we had no television reception and nowhere to swim. We tried not having any TV but ended up bringing videos. The best part about only having videos was that I could say one movie and then to bed— and that was that. It was quite a few years before satellite came to Columbia County and we liked it that way. The lack of a pool, on the other hand, was a bit more difficult. We knew that there are a lot of lakes in the area, but finding where to swim was not easy. There was no internet, and it was mostly a frustrating goose chase.

We joined the Egremont Country Club in nearby Massachusetts because they had a pool and it was only twenty minutes from the house. However, the pool was spring-fed, which meant that it was freezing cold, so Zach refused to even put his feet in the water. Plus, packing up the stuff for all of us took so much time that it was not even worth the effort.

Owen, Mom, Me, Zach and Dad

The second summer, we put in a pool. Toby was only fifteen months old when we put it in, and the last part of the work was the fence. He was the fastest running toddler in history, so the time it took for him to run from the house to the pool was about five seconds. I cannot tell you how many times we realized that he was in the pool. Oh my God, the most frightening thing ever! However, he learned to swim very quickly!

Living in the Hudson Valley had a lot of perks, and one of our outings that first summer was discovering the abundance of fruit farms. It was thrilling to find fresh local fruit—like cherries, apricots, peaches, and blueberries. Zach had a very significant sweet tooth, and it was not easy getting him to try new things. But during that first summer we came home from Love Apple Farm in Ghent with tons of cherries, which I made into an Eastern European cold cherry soup. Zach loved it, and the funny thing is—he married a woman from Poland whose family makes it for him whenever he is there.

COLD CHERRY SOUP

INGREDIENTS

3 lemons, zested and juiced

1/4 cup honey, or to taste

2 1/2 lbs. fresh cherries, sweet and/or sour, pitted (set aside about a dozen)

5 cups of water

1 tsp. ground cinnamon

1/2 cup of white wine

1 cup sour cream

DIRECTIONS

Place the lemon zest, lemon juice, honey, cherries, cinnamon, and water in a medium pot and bring to a boil. Turn down the heat and simmer for about 20 minutes or until the cherries are very soft, and then add the wine. Allow to cool and then blend until smooth in a blender or with an immersion blender. Stir in the sour cream and refrigerate until chilled. Serve with a few fresh cherries on top.

SERVES 4–6

Our relative seclusion on Dawson Road ended when Michelle, the mom of Zach's friend, Carly, mentioned to me that her friend lived both in Larchmont and in Columbia County. Laurie and her son, Jimmy, (along with husband, Phil) lived only three blocks from us in Larchmont and one town south in Copake in the country. Jimmy and Zach became fast friends, and I was very grateful to have a friend nearby whenever we were in the country. I recently learned that Carly now lives with her own family in the town just north of us, Chatham. I have not run into her yet (not that I would recognize her now).

Phil was a hamburger manufacturer in Manhattan, and they enjoyed cooking and eating good food as much as we did. They were also gardeners—serious gardeners, especially for tomatoes. They spent much of their summer in the garden and canned their bumper crop of tomatoes for their larder for the rest of the year. I have never been confident enough in my canning abilities to "put up" my tomatoes. I have always preferred to use whatever I could and freeze the rest.

But summers are short in Hillsdale, and there were always plenty of green tomatoes still on the vine when the weather got colder. It was always sad to leave our utopian lives in the Berkshires and head back to Westchester. As a farewell to summer, I often made green tomato chutney with the last of the crop, but our favorite treat was fried green tomatoes, served over creamy, delicious, cheesy grits.

FRIED GREEN TOMATOES
OVER CHEESE GRITS

INGREDIENTS

2 Tbs. unsalted butter

1 small yellow onion, finely
chopped

2 cups water

1/2 tsp. sea salt

1/2 cup white corn meal (grits)

1 tsp. Tabasco sauce

Freshly ground black pepper,
six turns

1 3/4 cups grated cheddar
cheese

3 Tbs. unsalted butter, softened

2 egg whites

4–5 large green tomatoes,
thickly sliced

2 tsp. sea salt and 1/2 tsp.
black pepper

1/2 cup all-purpose flour

1/2 cup all-purpose flour

4 Tbs. unsalted butter

DIRECTIONS

Preheat the oven to 400°. Melt the 2 Tbs. of butter in a small skillet over medium heat and sauté the onions until translucent, about 4 or 5 minutes. Bring the water to a boil in a 1-quart saucepan over high heat and add the salt, and then slowly pour in the grits while the water continues to boil. Boil for a minute, stirring constantly, then reduce the heat to medium and cook another 2 minutes. Add the onions, Tabasco, black pepper, 1 1/2 cups of the cheese, and the butter—and mix thoroughly. Butter a 1-quart casserole dish. Whisk the egg whites until stiff and fold them into the grits. Pour the grits into the dish and top with the remaining cheese. Bake for half an hour or until puffed and brown. Meanwhile, season the flour with the salt and pepper and place in a pie pan. Lightly coat the tomato slices with the seasoned flour. Add the butter to a medium-sized skillet over moderate heat until it is melted and sizzling. Add the tomatoes, without overcrowding them. Brown on the bottom and then carefully turn to brown on the second side. Transfer to a platter. Serve the tomatoes on top of the servings of cheese grits.

SERVES 4–6

Summer is the absolute best time in the Hudson Valley/ Berkshires. There are concerts everywhere, with Tanglewood being the biggest draw. There is music, dance, theatre, and every other cultural event possible. I believe that you could see a different show every night and never repeat a performance. We took the kids to see every genre—from Shakespeare to Indian dance, to jazz and everything in between.

Aside from the culture, it was nature that drew us to the area. There are lakes for swimming in the summer, skiing right down the road in the winter, amazing leaves to admire in the autumn, and lots and lots of mud in the spring! Spring is not a great time for much, except maple sugaring. We have a lot of sugar maples, including a huge maple tree shading our deck. One year, we hung up a few buckets and then headed south to Larchmont. About a week later, I asked Adam to come up with me to collect the sap.

We filled an entire plastic recycling trash can with the sap, put it in the back of the Volkswagen van and drove the two hours back home. Less than a mile from home, I made a sharp right turn and the bin tipped over and opened, spilling all the sap onto the floor of the van. The sap hit the engine and it smelled like maple syrup for a week every time we turned the engine on.

When we did succeed in making the syrup, which requires forty times the amount of sap, we enjoyed the northern tradition of "maple on snow." To make it, you boil maple syrup until it reaches a "soft ball" stage and pour it onto snow to create taffy. You then eat the taffy with donuts and homemade cucumber pickles—great fun!

CUCUMBER PICKLES

INGREDIENTS

2 lbs. small fresh cucumbers, washed thoroughly

2 Tbs. kosher salt

1 whole garlic bulb, peeled

1 small bunch of fresh dill

2 slices fresh white bread

DIRECTIONS

Fill a large, clean, glass jar halfway with cold water. Add enough salt to make the water quite salty (about 2 Tbs. for each liter of water). Pour the water into a large bowl. Stack the cucumber tightly into the jar. Pour the water on top and then add the garlic cloves and dill, and top off with the bread. Close the jar and place in a sunny spot for about 5 days or until the pickles have gone from bright green to dull green. Remove the bread and refrigerate.

As the boys grew older, their weekend commitments for sports or school events and synagogue obligations in Larchmont precluded our going up to the country for weeks, or even months, at a time. There were seasons that came and went without the time to get away. Those were very busy times with three boys, so when we were able to go somewhere, we chose to travel so that we had their undivided attention.

We continued to consider the house in the country our getaway place and never really thought of it as a place where we could live full-time. Peter still worked in New Jersey, and a commute from there to Hillsdale was impossible. We did not know about the Waldorf school right up the road, which would have been a wonderful school for the boys. We had no idea that such a magically creative place existed only six minutes from the house. So, we continued to live in Larchmont and came to the country just to get away.

Peter's parents bought a house on Sanibel Island on the west coast of Florida, and it was their refuge in their last years. We also had the great fortune of using the house when we needed a true getaway. It was sitting right on a fantastic beach with a pool and a community tennis court and a nature preserve. We went down there about twice a year, starting when Toby was a toddler.

We would go there as an entourage, with the three boys and our cat, Smudge, and we even brought Rampati with us a few times. It was heaven! We would get off the plane in Fort Meyers, stop at a fantastic green market near the airport for Florida produce, and then go to Jerry's supermarket for all the rest of the groceries needed for our week away. There were parrots in cages at the market and amazingly delicious and caloric apple fritters and key lime tarts at the bakery.

There could not have been a more perfect place to revamp and restore; as we would spend the days at the beach and in the pool, mostly cooking at home (often with Rampati there to clean up) and eating out when we needed a break. I was often inspired by the local ingredients to prepare meals featuring key limes. I enjoyed making Cuban black beans with white rice called *Moros y Cristianos*, which is a reference to the white Christians and the black slaves in Cuba.

MOROS Y CRISTIANOS—
CUBAN BLACK BEANS AND WHITE RICE

INGREDIENTS

1 lb. dried black beans
4 cups water
3 cloves garlic, minced
1 medium green bell pepper,
   diced
1 medium yellow onion, diced
1/4 lb. salt pork, chopped
1 lb. smoked ham hocks, cut
   into 1-inch pieces
1 Tbs. sweet paprika
1 Tbs. ground cumin
2 Bay leaves
4 cups chicken stock
2 Tbs. red wine vinegar
Salt and black pepper, to taste
Key limes
Medium-grain white rice,
   cooked according to
   directions on package

DIRECTIONS

Wash the beans and place them in a medium pot and add the water. Bring to a boil and then turn off the heat and allow the beans to soak for an hour. Add the rest of the ingredients (except the vinegar, rice, and Key lime) and cook covered on medium-low heat for about 2 hours or until the beans are soft. Add the vinegar and taste for seasoning. Serve hot with the white rice with Key lime juice squeezed on top.

SERVES 4–6

Peter and Adam on Sanibel

Right about the time when we were the busiest with the kids, Peter's mother became very ill with cancer and required much of his attention. She had esophageal cancer and suffered for two years until it metastasized to her spine. It was March, and we knew her end was near, but it was also close to Toby's fourth birthday, and I prayed that she would wait until April 1st. However, she passed on his birthday, March 31st, at the age of sixty-seven.

Less than a week later, Peter's father had prostate surgery and had a serious stroke a couple of days after that. Those were very difficult times and required Peter to be caring first for his mother and then his father. His father slowly recovered some of his speech and some of his movement. However, two years into his slow and arduous recovery he had a second stroke and died at the age of sixty-nine. I must admit that at the time I thought they were old! I guess old age really is all relative. Here I am, close to their ages, and it is not old!

Peter's parents lived in a very large modern house overlooking the beach on Long Island Sound. The house had six bedrooms, five bathrooms, and a pool. It was in the same elementary school district as where our kids were attending. We decided that we would sell our house and move into their home, and we were set to move in July.

I had decided earlier in the year that I wanted to finally have my Bat Mitzvah. Although it is most common for a young Jewish girl or boy to have the ceremony upon reaching adulthood (thirteen), my parents were not members of a synagogue and they were not interested in the celebration. When I asked them for one, they responded that my great-grandfather would not have approved. I can't believe I didn't put up a fight, but I didn't, so I guess it really wasn't that important to me at the time.

I had been waiting for many years for life to be a little less complicated and for a rabbi with whom I would feel comfortable studying Torah as an adult. That rabbi came in the form of Rabbi Camille Angel. When I asked her if we could prepare for my Bat Mitzvah, she asked me when I was thinking of having it, and we looked up the Torah portion for that week. It was at the end of June and my birthday would be in July, when I would be turning thirty-eight.

The Torah portion for the week that I chose began, "After thirty-eight years of wandering in the desert, the Israelites came to the Promised Land." That was a sign to me that this was the right time with the right rabbi. We studied together once a week or so, and I really enjoyed the challenge.

However, as the date approached, Peter's father was at the end of his life, and we knew that we would be moving into their house soon after. I decided to have my Bat Mitzvah on Iselin Terrace in the early evening and asked all the guests to bring dessert, as it was a dessert-only party. I read my Torah portion easily, and our boys participated adorably—and everything was going according to plan when one of the guests found out that OJ Simpson was being chased by the police. The television was turned on and many of the guests spent the rest of the time watching the chase.

For the rest of us, we had a great time tasting everyone's delicious desserts and ignored the television as best as we could. My friend Liz was the best cook I had ever had the great fortune to know, and she brought with her a lemon pound cake like nothing I had ever tasted. It is still the very best cake of its kind.

LEMON POUND CAKE

INGREDIENTS

2 sticks unsalted butter, softened

2 cups white sugar

2 cups white flour, sifted

1 Tbs. lemon juice

1 tsp. vanilla extract

5 extra-large eggs, at room temperature

1 cup confectioner's sugar

1 Tbs. lemon juice

DIRECTIONS

Preheat oven to 350°. Spray a Bundt pan thoroughly with nonstick spray. In an electric mixer, cream the butter and sugar for about 5 minutes, or until light yellow and fluffy. Add the flour to the mixer and mix well. Add the lemon juice and vanilla and mix in completely. Add the eggs, one at a time, mixing well after each addition. Pour into the Bundt pan. Bake for 75 minutes or until a toothpick emerges clean from the batter. Cool in the pan for 10 minutes. Meanwhile, put the confectioner's sugar in a small bowl and add just enough lemon juice to make a paste. Turn the pan over onto a cooling rack and remove the cake from the pan. Poke the cake all over using a toothpick, and then pour the glaze over the cake and allow to cool completely.

SERVES 8–10

A week or two after my celebration, we packed up our things and moved to 47 Magnolia Avenue, the house where Peter grew up. Despite our continued desire to live in Hillsdale, in July of 1994 we left the house on Iselin Terrace after twelve years and moved our full-time residence to Magnolia Avenue.

My Bat Mitzvah: Rabbi Larry Hoffman and me

CHAPTER 9

47 MAGNOLIA AVENUE
LARCHMONT, NEW YORK
JULY 1994–APRIL 2001

This was a big house; I mean big! There were five bedrooms, six bathrooms; and every room was decorated in my mother-in-law's taste. For the first month or so, I was in shock and unable to do very much. I found it very difficult to even unpack the boxes. I was overwhelmed by the amount of work it would take to make this house my home.

Even the kitchen window was not designed for me; it was so high that I could not see out of it. I had to use a step stool to see the backyard from the kitchen sink. On the first day, we pushed aside the long drapes, curtains, and shades on the living room window, and—lo and behold—we could see the Long Island Sound. We had no idea that there were views of the water because every window had been covered. The house was a block from the sound, with the town beach right there for us to enjoy!

In addition, the park along the water was beautiful and inviting. That first summer, while I was busy unpacking, the boys would go down to the beach and order lunch or go for walks in the park. Plus, we had our own pool in the backyard. It really was heaven! The only downside was that the boys did not know the neighborhood kids, and this was not like Iselin Terrace—there was literally no one outside playing in their yards. That took some getting used to.

We went to the beach every chance we could, and the boys would spend the time swimming, building sand castles, and finding sea creatures, such as hermit crabs, jellyfish, and horseshoe crabs. We often ordered lunch at the little beach shack, which was run by a retired Larchmont policeman named Ralph. He was a nice guy but had absolutely no experience in or any sense of how to run a food business. The teenage boy at the grill would take one order at a time, so if there were six people waiting on line for burgers, you would have to wait until each person's burger was finished before yours was put on the grill—*just ridiculous!* On the other hand, Ralph's Italian salad with tuna was absolutely delicious, and we ordered it every time we were there.

I would often pack up a lunch of leftovers from dinner the night before. When I was organized enough in the morning to plan for lunch, I would make cold soup to bring to the beach. I love cold cucumber yogurt soup, cold leek and potato soup, cold beet borscht, and cold cherry soup—but I can never get enough gazpacho, and it was one of the quickest preparations I knew. All the great summer vegetables are thrown into the blender with lots of seasonings, and it's done.

THE BEST GAZPACHO

INGREDIENTS

8 medium garden-ripe
   tomatoes, cut into quarters
4 Kirby cucumbers, peeled and
   cut into large chunks
1 green bell pepper, seeded
   and cut into large pieces
1 sweet onion (Vidalia or
   similar), peeled and cut into
   quarters
1 clove garlic, peeled and cut
   in half
2-inch slice of French bread,
   cut into chunks
1–2 cups of cold water, amount
   depends on juiciness of
   tomatoes
4 Tbs. extra-virgin olive oil
4 Tbs. red wine vinegar
1 Tbs. salt
1 1/2 tsp. sweet paprika
1/2 tsp. ground cumin
Fresh ground black pepper
Garnish with chopped fresh
   Haas-type avocado, cut into
   small pieces (Thanks, Judy!)

DIRECTIONS

Put half or a third of each of the ingredients into a blender or food processor fitted with the metal blade and process until no very large chunks remain, but do not make a puree. Pour this mixture into a large bowl. Repeat the process. When all the mixtures are combined in the bowl, give it a good stir and taste it for seasoning. (I like it very well seasoned.) Refrigerate for at least 2 hours, taste again for seasoning and serve garnished with the chopped avocado.

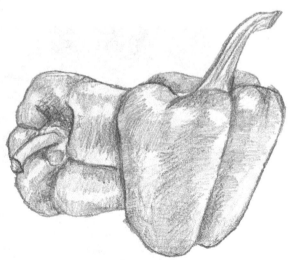

When Adam was ten years old, we signed him up for the Reform Jewish camp right near us in the country, in Great Barrington, Massachusetts. Our friend's son had been going to Camp Eisner for a few years already, and the family spoke of nothing else all year. There was also a day camp on the grounds for younger kids, so we signed Zach and Toby up for that as well. We spent the summer in the country, with Peter commuting and the younger guys at day camp. I had time to myself for the first time since Adam was born.

It was at camp that I met Susan, the wife of the rabbi from Larchmont Temple, who had three sons going to Eisner Day Camp with Zach and Toby. Her husband was on the staff at the camp for a couple of weeks, and she and I became friends. Her oldest sons were twins who were Zach's age, and the younger son was Toby's age. At the end of the summer, we came back home to Magnolia Avenue, and I was so surprised and delighted to see Susan standing outside her home right around the corner from us. I would not have guessed how we would become such good friends!

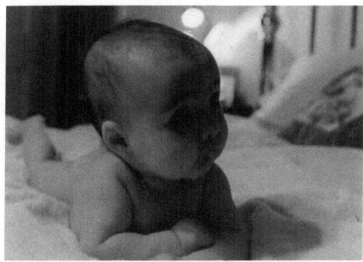

Elizabeth at six weeks

Catty-corner from our house on Magnolia was a house that was rented out, and one day a new family moved in. They had an adorable one-year-old daughter named Emily, who grabbed me by the heart with great longing for a little girl. Peter and I began discussing the idea of having another child—boy or girl! I mentioned this idea to Susan, who said that she and her husband, Jeffrey, were having the same conversation. We found out on the same day that we were pregnant, and months later found out the results from the amnio reports that we were both having girls! The girls were born the same day!

Our daughter, Elizabeth Jane, was born at 10:00 a.m. on July 2nd, after a planned Cesarean section. I had wanted her to be born on July 4th so that there would be fireworks every year for her birthday, but the doctor told me that they don't schedule surgeries on holidays. She was a healthy, beautiful child and we were overjoyed at having a delightful little girl after three incredible boys. We decided to hold the baby naming for her at the end of the summer, because our rabbi had the summer off and I needed time to recover from the surgery.

Susan and her family held their baby-naming ceremony for Sophie a week after she was born. We had both had had Cesarean sections, and it was a big deal for me to make it to their house for the ceremony, as it was my first solo outing with Elizabeth. It took all my strength to get there, but it was at their party that I tasted my first whitefish salad, and it remains one of my favorite brunch treats of all time.

SMOKED WHITEFISH SALAD

INGREDIENTS

1/2 lb. smoked whitefish, skinned, bones carefully removed
1 celery stalk, finely chopped
1 scallion, finely chopped
1–2 Tbs. mayonnaise
1 Tbs. whipped cream cheese
1 Tbs. sour cream
1 tsp. fresh dill, finely chopped
Salt and pepper, to taste

DIRECTIONS

Combine all ingredients— carefully, so as not to mash the whitefish.

Six days after Elizabeth was born, I turned forty and was slowly recovering. I took a shower, and when I came out of the bathroom, I was truly surprised by a group of friends with a luncheon on the deck outside our bedroom. It was quite a shock! I was truly touched and grateful, but so exhausted.

We invited all our family, friends, and the members of our synagogue (our Chavurah) to the baby naming at the end of August. Our student rabbi, Camille Angel, was on hand to perform the ceremony—and our friends, Merri and Ramie, who were members of the Chavurah, played guitar and led the singing masterfully. At one point, Ramie was holding Elizabeth while Camille was blessing her, and I could see the look on Elizabeth's face changed from amused to serious. As her mother, I knew what that look meant; she was pooping right there in Ramie's arms. Luckily, no one else (including Ramie) seemed to notice, and the diaper held, but it was quite hysterical!

After the ceremony, we served brunch and thankfully, I had hired a woman named Brenda to cater the event. She was a gifted kosher caterer from nearby, and everything was delicious. However, I was in such a daze that the only dish I can remember was a wonderful creation of bulgur wheat and red cabbage. It remains one of my go-to dishes when I, myself, cater.

BRENDA'S CONFETTI SALAD

INGREDIENTS

1 cup medium bulgur wheat, soaked in cold water to cover for 1 hour

1 cup thinly sliced red cabbage

1 cup coarsely grated carrots

1 cup seedless grapes

1/2 cup red bell pepper, sliced thinly

1/2 cup radishes, sliced thinly

1/2 cup frozen green peas, defrosted

1/2 cup scallions, chopped

1/2 cup toasted pumpkin seeds

Dressing

1/4 cup white wine vinegar

Juice of 1 lemon

4 Tbs. honey

2 Tbs. olive oil

2 Tbs. tamari soy sauce

1 Tbs. toasted sesame oil

1 tsp. Dijon mustard

1 Tbs. toasted sesame seeds

DIRECTIONS

Drain the bulgur and squeeze dry in a cloth towel. Toss the bulgur with the remaining salad ingredients. Mix the dressing ingredients together in a small bowl and then toss into the salad.

SERVES 6

Not long after we moved into the house on Magnolia Avenue, we learned that the beach on Sanibel was eroding. Captiva Island, which is over the bridge from Sanibel had recently completed a beach restoration program that pulled the sand from Sanibel's beaches and caused catastrophic changes in the coastline. We flew down to Florida with the kids and arrived at the house to see the Gulf of Mexico literally lapping at the window; it was horrifying!

Peter hired a coastal engineer who looked over the situation and told us that we must begin to rebuild the entire beach, or all the homes would be washed away. The city of Sanibel was not interested in this project, nor was the state of Florida. Peter decided that we and the neighbors would sue the city and the state, arguing that the fresh water system, which was very close to the shoreline, would be destroyed if nothing was done to correct the situation.

They won the case, but it would take too long to get the funding from the city and state, so the neighbors agreed to fund the beach restoration themselves. Eventually, the city continued to rebuild the shoreline, but our engineer told us to sell the house before the next big hurricane. At that point, Elizabeth was a few months old, and we all went down to be in the house one last time.

Last visit to Sanibel

My parents were in Miami at the time, and they drove up with my dad's sister, Blanche, and her husband, Seymour, to visit for lunch. I prepared a typical Cuban meal in honor of their daughter-in-law, Sonia. Sonia married my cousin, Fred, and we were thrilled to include her and her traditions to the family. (We are still close and still swapping recipes.) I made plantains with mojo; chicken with garlic; and Moros y Cristianos, black beans with white rice. I had enjoyed the plantains with mojo at Sonia and Freddy's wedding a few years earlier.

PLANTAINS WITH MOJO

INGREDIENTS

3 green plantains
Ice water
2 cups vegetable oil
3 garlic cloves, peeled
1 tsp. kosher salt
1 tsp. freshly ground black
   pepper
3 limes, squeezed
1/2 cup extra-virgin olive oil
Dash of hot pepper sauce

DIRECTIONS

Cut off the ends of the plantains and score the peel down the ridges with a sharp knife. Peel the plantains and slice lengthwise as thinly as possible, using a mandolin or the slicing blade of a food processor. Place the slices into an ice water bath for a few minutes. Meanwhile, heat the oil in a large frying pan until it reaches a temperature of 350°. Combine the garlic, salt and pepper in a small bowl. Add the lime juice, olive oil, and hot pepper sauce to taste and combine well as a condiment for the plantains. Blot the plantain slices on paper towels and fry a handful at a time in the hot oil until they are golden and crisp on both sides. Drain and serve with the mojo sauce.

Sadly, we had to sell the house once we were able to restore the beach. At the time, we had the house in Larchmont with a pool and the house in the country with a pool, so it seemed way over the top to also own a house in Sanibel with a pool. We were really very lucky to live that life, but at the time it was all too overwhelming. I was stretched as far as I could go, trying to keep up with all the kids' needs physically and emotionally.

Once Elizabeth started nursery school, I was driving the four of them to four different schools at pretty much the same time. After school, there were play rehearsals, soccer practice, ballet class, play dates, PTA meetings, and all the myriad of other activities expected of an affluent Westchester kid times four. I did my best to get everyone where they had to go within a reasonable amount of time and keep them fed and clothed. Home-cooked dinners was what really suffered through this—along with, I see now, the time and focus to address some other important factors in their emotional lives. Mea culpa!

Whenever possible, I cooked for them but also for myself. The kitchen has always been my refuge and has the dual function of soothing me and providing nourishment for my family. I recall one Sunday afternoon when every child was busy somewhere else, and I had a few hours to myself in the kitchen. Ever since visiting New Orleans as a teenager, I was in love with Creole/Cajun cuisine. I made a cauldron of gumbo that served as dinner, then leftovers, and then lunch, with a few additions each time to vary the flavors and textures.

CHICKEN AND ANDOUILLE GUMBO

INGREDIENTS

8 chicken wings, washed, dried, and seasoned with salt and pepper
5 Tbs. vegetable oil
4 Tbs. flour
2 quarts chicken stock, warmed
2 bay leaves
2 dried red peppers
2 tsp. fresh thyme
1 large onion, chopped
2 garlic cloves, minced
1 Andouille sausage, sliced
1/2 pound fresh or frozen okra, sliced
1 large green bell pepper, chopped
1 tsp. cayenne, or to taste
1 tsp. hot pepper sauce, or to taste
1 Tbs. ground sassafras (optional)
1 lemon, juiced
Hot steamed white rice

DIRECTIONS

Heat a large soup pot over medium-high heat, and when hot add 1 Tbs. of the oil. When the oil is hot, add the chicken and brown on both sides. Remove the chicken from the pot and add the rest of the oil. When the oil is hot, add the flour and turn the heat to low. Stir the roux constantly until it becomes a deep brown (about 5 or so minutes). Add the bay leaves, dried peppers, onions, garlic, okra, and green pepper—and stir for about 5 minutes or until the vegetables have softened. Now add the stock in a slow, steady stream, stirring all the while. Return the chicken to the pot and add the cayenne and hot pepper sauce. Bring to a boil and then turn the heat to low and partially cover. Cook for one hour and then add the sassafras. Allow to sit covered for 10 minutes and then add the lemon juice and taste for seasoning. Add rice to empty bowls and serve the gumbo on top.

SERVES 8

In theory, the house on Magnolia should have been a dream, but reality was different. The house was never my house; it would always be my mother-in-law's, so the first thing I did to put my mark on it was to paint murals on the walls. I painted a scene of Australia on Zach's walls, a scene of Africa on Toby's walls, a Native American scene in the kid's bathroom. This did transform the spaces to some extent, but the memories of Pat and Ed lingered and hung over every room.

Driving the kids everywhere they needed to go left little time to prepare dinner. We were often eating take-in food from local restaurants and ate it in the few minutes between pick-ups and drop-offs. Luckily, there were some very good choices around us, and take-in became one of our routines. There was a really excellent Thai restaurant nearby, and the owner, an older woman, had a real crush on Zach, which was very sweet. We often enjoyed their food both at the restaurant and at home. No matter what Thai food we ordered for our dinners, we always ordered the same thing for dessert; mango with sticky rice. I still put it in the category of best dessert because it is sweet and tart and creamy and nutty and not too bad for you!

MANGO WITH STICKY RICE

INGREDIENTS

2 cups sticky (sweet) rice, soaked in cold water for half an hour

2 cans light coconut milk, shaken

1 cup sugar

1 tsp. sea salt

3 ripe mangoes, peeled and sliced

1 tsp. toasted sesame seeds

DIRECTIONS

Place the rice into a rice cooker and add enough water to cover the rice by 1 inch. When the rice cooker finishes the cooking stage, check to make sure the rice is not dry, adding water if needed. If not using a rice cooker, place the soaked rice in a medium saucepan and cover with water by one inch. Bring to a boil, then lower the heat, cover, and cook for twenty minutes or until the rice is cooked. Add a small amount of warm water if the rice looks dry. Meanwhile, place the coconut milk, sugar, and salt in a medium saucepan and cook over moderate heat for 15 minutes or until thickened. Mix the sticky rice with 2 cups of the coconut milk. Put the rice on a serving dish. Place the mangoes on top of the rice. Pour the rest of the coconut milk on top, sprinkle with sesame seeds, and serve immediately.

SERVES 4

One of the wonderful attributes of the house on Magnolia was that it was well-designed for parties. My in-laws hosted parties on a regular basis, as did my parents, so I was programmed for it. Soon after we finished the redesigning and painting of the house, we held a housewarming party. I hired a caterer I had met at the kid's school and invited about fifty friends—and it was a great party.

The most exciting revelation as a result of this party was that I felt there was no reason why I could not cater as well, if not better, than all the caterers I had hired over the years. This idea stayed with me for years until I finally catered my first party, about twelve years after the housewarming party—but more about that in the final chapter.

We celebrated Adam's Bar Mitzvah in the backyard at Magnolia in September of the first year that we were in the house. Three years after that, Zach had his Bar Mitzvah at the house. The rooms all flowed one into the other in such a fashion that people could spread out throughout the house and into the backyard with ease. We hosted over a hundred people at these events and it never felt crowded.

We continued to maintain our membership in the Chavurah over those years, but soon after moving to Magnolia, we decided to also join Larchmont Temple. My friend Susan's husband, Jeff, was the rabbi there and we thought it would be nice to belong to our local synagogue. Peter's parents were founding members, and there was a youth group, which we thought would be good for the boys to join.

What we didn't think about was that both the Chavurah and the Temple would be celebrating holidays at the exact same time, making us have to choose one over the other every time. We ended up giving up the Temple membership, but they permitted the kids to continue in the youth group and with Confirmation.

We preferred the intimacy of the Chavurah, as there were only twenty-five families, compared to the thousand or so at the Temple. One of my favorite traditions in the Chavurah was that in the evening when we welcomed the New Year, Rosh Hashanah, there was a sweets table for all the participants. During the High Holidays, there were not only the twenty-five families but also extended families and many guests. The tables were overflowing with sweets in the hope for a sweet New Year. I almost always brought an apple cake because it is traditional to dip apples in honey for the holiday but also because the cake is so very simple to make. Making it for eighty is as easy as making it for eight—and it is a simple pleasure to eat. Jewish desserts are often simple and *haimish* (homey).

ROSH HASHANAH APPLE CAKE

INGREDIENTS

6-8 apples
1/2 cup apricot jam
1/4 cup honey
1 Tbs. butter
3 eggs
1/2 cup canola oil
3/4 cup sugar
2 tsp. baking powder
1 cup A.P. flour
1 tsp. vanilla extract
Confectioner's sugar or
   whipped cream.

DIRECTIONS

Preheat oven to 350°. Grease a deep 9-inch cake pan. Peel and slice the apples. Place into the greased pan. Melt the jam, honey, and butter together and pour on top of the fruit. Beat the eggs and then add the oil and sugar. When it is well mixed, add the baking powder and flour. Mix well and add the vanilla. Pour the batter on top of the fruit and bake for 1 hour. After 55 minutes check center of cake with a toothpick. Bake until toothpick comes out clean. Allow to cool for 10 minutes and then loosen the sides of the cakes with a knife. Invert the cake onto a serving plate (tap with the knife if it seems to be sticking to the pan). Sprinkle with confectioner's sugar or top with whipped cream.

SERVES 6-8

Peter had worked at the family factory in New Jersey from the week we graduated college and had slowly risen from broom sweeper to president of the company. The business manufactured plastic and metal packaging for the watch and jewelry industry. Peter's great-grandfather was Joseph Bulova, and Joseph's daughter, Julia, started the company to make boxes for their watches. However, over time, most of the customers moved their own manufacturing from the United States to China. One by one, the company lost all of their major accounts: Longine, Citizen, Pulsar, Seiko, and then one day, their founding customer, Bulova.

Losing the Bulova account was the final straw, and Peter was forced to close the factory that had been in the family for one hundred years. It was a very sad time for him, and firing all these people was the hardest thing he ever had to do. He had not taken a salary for over two years, we had three kids in private school, and the taxes on our house were insane. We had a quarter-acre property, and we paid more than $45,000 in annual taxes on it.

We made the difficult decision after seven years in his parents' house to move to a less expensive neighborhood. It took over two years with over one hundred showings (straightening up a house with four kids, including a three-year-old, before each showing) until we finally sold the house.

CHAPTER 10

1 LANCIA LANE
LARCHMONT, NEW YORK
MAY 2000–JUNE 2006

After a great deal of searching, we finally found an interesting house with five bedrooms, four bathrooms, and a small but lovely yard in a pretty neighborhood. The kitchen had a large window over the sink looking out into the very narrow backyard. It was a couple of blocks from a nature trail and close to town. This house met all of our requirements at a price we could afford. The reason it was affordable was that it was in the part of town where the elementary school was 40 percent Latinx.

We had left the elementary school where Peter went as a child, as did his mother. It claimed to be "international," which was true but only because the children of United Nations diplomats were students there. We were excited for Elizabeth to meet children who were not as privileged as those in our former home's school.

However, this was not the attitude that we encountered when we told people where she was going. Elizabeth's nursery-school friend's mom asked me which school she would be attending in the fall, and when I told her Elizabeth would be going to Mamaroneck Avenue School, she said, "Oh, that's where my cleaning woman's son goes." *So obnoxious* . . .

Elizabeth and Toby, first day of school, Lancia Lane

What I did not know was the level of devotion to these children of new immigrants I would find in the teachers and the administration. Spanish was the language spoken at home for these children, and English was pretty much only spoken at school. Bringing the English competency level up, compared to the other elementary schools in the district, was the school's number one priority.

The previous elementary school that the boys had attended had put the emphasis on creativity and developmental readiness for academics. Mamaroneck Avenue School put the three R's (reading, writing, arithmetic) front and center. There was plenty of nurturing and relationship-building between the school and the home, but class time was strictly monitored for the number of hours devoted to classic learning.

My favorite event at MAS was the International Fair in the spring. At this school, international was just that—new immigrants from everywhere came with their children to this school, and they all represented their mother countries at different booths at the fair. Beginning our first year, I took on the volunteer position as coordinator for the food from the community to be served for lunch.

Parents would come to me with enormous trays of home-cooked specialties from Columbia, Mexico, El Salvador, Puerto Rico, and so many other countries.

I knew that many of these people worked as cleaning women, day laborers, and countless other low-paying jobs to make ends meet—and yet they were so thrilled to bring mountains of their delicious food to share with the community. It was thrilling to be in charge of accepting it and serving it to everyone.

We had been visiting Puerto Rico annually as a family for a number of years and so I was very familiar with the cuisine. One of the moms brought in her tray of chicken and rice from Puerto Rico, called *asopao de pollo*. It was always a favorite of mine whenever we were in San Juan, and I was so excited to offer it for the fair.

CHICKEN ASOPAO

INGREDIENTS

1 large (3-lb.) chicken, cut in 1/8ths, or 3 lbs. of chicken pieces of choice

3 garlic cloves, put through a garlic press

1 tsp. fresh or 1/2 tsp. dried oregano

2 tsp. kosher salt and 1/2 tsp. freshly ground black pepper

2 Tbs. olive oil

1 cup white wine

1 large onion, chopped

1 green pepper, chopped

1/4 lb. chorizo sausage, thinly sliced

1 1/2 cups short-grain white rice

16 oz. can chopped tomatoes

8 cups chicken stock

1/2 cup frozen green peas, defrosted

1/4 cup pimiento-stuffed green olives

1 Tbs. capers

1/4 cup fresh cilantro, chopped coarsely

DIRECTIONS

Combine the garlic, oregano, salt, pepper, and 1 Tbs. of the olive oil in a small bowl to form a paste. Rub the chicken all over with the paste and allow to marinate for half an hour. In a large, heavy pot that has a lid, heat the remaining tablespoon of olive oil over medium heat. Add the chicken, taking care not to overcrowd, and brown evenly on all sides, removing the pieces to a plate as they brown. Add the wine and stir off all the brown pieces on the bottom of the pot with a spoon. Add the onion, peppers, and rice—and cook for 5 minutes. Add the tomatoes and bring to a simmer. Return the chicken to the pot and add the stock. Bring to a simmer, then turn down the heat and cook, partially covered, for twenty minutes, stirring occasionally. Taste for seasoning, add the peas, olives, capers, and cilantro—and cook for 5 more minutes.

SERVES 6

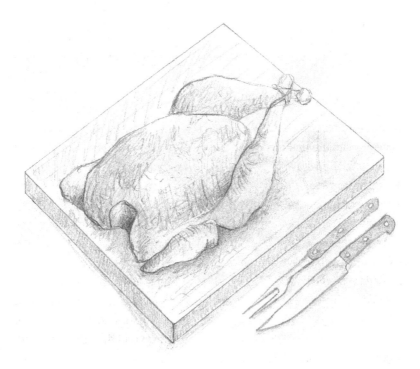

One of the features of the fair was the silent auction room. Parents offered goods and services with a sign-up sheet in front of the offering. One year, Elizabeth decided to sign up for all the items she wanted without telling us. We won a lot of make-up, clothes, and other items that a nine-year-old desired but that we had not even thought to sign up for. It was pretty silly, but the fact that it was a fundraiser for this bare-bones school kept us from complaining. I had offered a gourmet catered dinner for four as an item one year. Our good friends Joy and Rick got the winning bid. They invited us to join them for the dinner, which I served in their backyard one summer evening. In addition to gazpacho with shrimp, I made a seafood paella. We all thoroughly enjoyed the evening.

CHICKEN AND CHORIZO PAELLA

INGREDIENTS

6 boneless, skinless chicken
thighs, cut into quarters

1 tsp. dried oregano

1 tsp. sweet paprika

1 tsp. smoked paprika

Kosher salt and freshly ground
black pepper

4 Tbs. extra-virgin olive oil

1 dried Spanish chorizo
sausage, sliced

3 large cloves garlic, minced

1 large sweet onion, diced

1 green bell or cubanelle
pepper, diced

1 red bell pepper, diced

2 cups of fresh or canned
chopped tomatoes

1 1/2 cups medium-grain rice

1/2 tsp. saffron, soaked in 1/4
cup warm water

4 cups warm chicken stock

1/2 cup frozen green peas,
defrosted

1/2 cup jarred piquillo red
peppers, cut into strips

1/2 lemon, sliced

DIRECTIONS

Preheat the oven to 425°. Rinse and dry the chicken and sprinkle with the oregano, paprika, salt, and pepper. Heat a paella pan with the olive oil over medium-high heat. Brown the chicken for about 5 minutes and then add the chorizo. Turn so that all the chicken has browned and then remove to a plate. Add the garlic, onion, green and red pepper—and sauté until softened. Add the tomatoes and then the rice. Add the saffron and then the stock and bring to a boil, stirring occasionally for about 7 minutes. Place in the oven and bake for about 15 minutes, checking to see if additional stock is needed if the rice is getting too dry. Remove from the oven and add the peas and piquillo peppers. Stir thoroughly. Serve with the lemon wedges.

SERVES 6

The back of our property had a wooden split-rail fence, and right on the other side of the fence was a house that was rented to foreign diplomats and their families. Soon after we moved in, we met our neighbors to the left, who were from Montreal and had a daughter a few years older than Elizabeth who loved to dance. The two girls got along instantly and created dance after dance together for all the years that we lived on Lancia Lane.

The house behind us was empty for a few months, but during the summer of 2001, a family from Paris moved in. Their daughter, Isis, was exactly Elizabeth's age, and we soon became friendly with the family. The husband was a Moroccan Jew and his wife, Nathalie, had converted to Judaism. We spent a nice amount of time with them and stayed in touch for a number of years. Elizabeth stayed with them when we visited Paris.

Elizabeth started full-day kindergarten in early September, and in anticipation of having some time on my hands, I decided to try to teach cooking from our home. A short time after school began, 9/11 happened—and the world turned upside down and inside out. I had already sent out flyers to promote my cooking classes, and I was certain no one would want to leave their homes to learn to cook. But the opposite was true; people were not eating out at restaurants and needed to learn more kitchen skills.

We invited Nathalie and her family to dinner one evening and she brought with her a recipe of her mother's, potatoes *dauphinoise*, and it has been a family favorite of ours and is included in every French cooking class that I teach. It is the ultimate comfort food— combining potatoes, cream, and Gruyere cheese. One of my sons has been known to enjoy it warmed up for breakfast.

NATHALIE'S POTATOES DAUPHINOISE

INGREDIENTS

8 russet potatoes, peeled and
quartered

4 shallots, peeled

1 1/2 cups Gruyere cheese,
grated

1 cup whole milk, or more if
needed

1 cup crème fraîche or sour
cream

4 Tbs. butter

Salt and fresh-ground black
pepper

DIRECTIONS

Preheat the oven to 375°. Butter a 9 x 12-inch shallow baking pan or gratin dish. Using the slicing blade of a food processor, a mandolin, or the slicing side of a four-sided grater, slice the potatoes and the shallots. Starting with the potatoes, layer the potatoes, shallots, cheese, crème fraîche, salt, and pepper—making about three layers, ending with the cheese. Pour in enough milk to come halfway up the side of the dish. Dot the top with the remaining butter. Cover with aluminum foil and bake for 45 minutes. Remove the foil and bake for another 45 minutes or until brown and crisp on top.

SERVES 4–6

I gave my first cooking class in our kitchen at the island we had installed to separate the kitchen from the dining room. It was a soup class featuring mushroom-barley soup, Ukrainian borscht, and vichyssoise. I had two students, both of whom were friends, and sadly, both have since passed away. I taught a few more classes after that at home and then an acquaintance of mine suggested that I offer my classes at the Continuing Education program at the high school.

I was immediately approved for the classes and taught evening classes in the high school Home Economics room for the next five years. They paid for all the advertising and promotion, which was a great advantage. It was very convenient teaching in that space, as it was well-equipped and large enough for me to teach as many as fifteen students. I needed to bring all my own supplies, but there were high-school students assigned to carry my bags up to the room and back down again. I always had full classes, and they paid very well—so all in all, it was a really good gig.

After a few years, our neighbors moved back to Paris, and we were certain that Elizabeth would never be so lucky as to have a buddy right in the backyard again. However, very soon after, a new family moved into that house, and they were from Norway. They had four daughters and a son. Their third daughter, Rebecca, was exactly Elizabeth's age, and they became fast friends.

The husband, Geir, worked at the Norwegian embassy, and his wife, Mona, had been working with a Palestinian relief agency during their previous assignment in East Jerusalem. We invited them to dinner one evening and Mona offered to bring dessert. She walked into the house with a chocolate cake in her hands and announced that it was the same cake that she made for Yasser Arafat. The comment hung heavily in the air the whole evening.

Mona loved to bake and she made delicious cardamom rolls, with and without chocolate chips, every week. Elizabeth spent many days at their home and enjoyed those rolls immensely. I later found out that they were the only food offered during the entire day. Needless to say, she always came home starving but happy. After a few years they moved back to Norway, and then Elizabeth begged us to go and visit them and so we went to Norway and enjoyed the scenery, the seafood, and especially the bread!

MONA'S NORWEGIAN CARDAMOM ROLLS

INGREDIENTS

1 stick unsalted butter
1 1/4 cup milk
2 tsp. freshly ground cardamom
2 Tbs. active dry yeast
3/4 cup sugar
1 egg
1/2 tsp. salt
4 1/2–5 cups flour
1 beaten egg, for brushing

DIRECTIONS

In a small saucepan, melt butter over medium heat. Add the milk and cardamom and heat until hot (don't bring it to a boil), then set aside and cool until it's lukewarm. In a large mixing bowl, stir 1/2 cup or so of the lukewarm milk and a Tbs. of the sugar into the yeast, using a wooden spoon. Let sit until the yeast bubbles, about 5 minutes. Pour in the remaining milk, along with the rest of the sugar and the egg and salt. Stir in the flour gradually, beginning with about half of the flour and then adding 1/2 cup or so at a time until you have a dough that's firm and releases from the sides of the bowl. Turn the dough onto a lightly floured surface and knead for 10 minutes. Gather the dough and form it into a large ball. Lightly grease a large bowl (you can minimize the dishes by wiping out and using the same mixing bowl you used to stir the dough). Plop in the dough, turning it around until it's coated with the oil. Cover with a damp cloth and set to rise in a warm place until doubled.

Preheat the oven to 425° and line two baking sheets with parchment. Punch down the dough and shape into 12 balls. Place them on the baking sheets, making sure the smoothest side is up. Cover with a damp towel and let rise again, this time about 20 minutes. Brush with the beaten egg. Bake in the center of the oven, one sheet at a time, for about 10 minutes until golden on top. Watch carefully, as the buns can quickly darken. Rotate the baking sheet if needed for even baking. If the buns are browning too quickly and the insides need additional baking time, then cover the tops with a sheet of aluminum foil. Cool on a wire rack.

YIELD: 12 ROLLS

In addition to teaching cooking classes at the high school, I also began to see clients in my long-neglected social work field. I was advising parents of children with learning differences through the Special Education process. I would help them to determine what needs their children had and which services the school district could provide for them. It was very rewarding but also very emotionally draining. Listening to the stories of the parents was often heartbreaking, and sometimes there was very little the school district could do to help. On the other hand, there were many times when I represented families at their Committee on Special Education meetings and was able to provide the children with the services they needed that they had not been successful securing before.

Soon after Elizabeth started at Mamaroneck Avenue School, I became involved in their Parent Teachers Association as a way to meet people and show support for the school. In addition to the elementary-school PTA I was also involved in district-wide programs. Two of our sons had received services from the Special Education department, so when the position of copresident of the Special Ed PTA for the district was available, I decided to take it on. I met with my cochair, Jennifer Bourdain, and we instantly clicked. She told me about her brother-in-law, Anthony, who was soon to become an internationally-famous chef. I had never heard of him then, but she gave me a book of his, *Kitchen Confidential*, which he had autographed for me.

We became friendly with Jennifer and her husband, Chris, and had them over for Passover Seder along with about six college friends of Adam's. It was a very boisterous and joyous evening, with all the college kids drinking Manischewitz wine. I believed that Chris and Jennifer were both Christian, so I mistakenly explained the meaning of everything at the Seder. A few years later, one of Anthony Bourdain's television episodes hinted that he was Jewish. Oops!

One evening, we went out to dinner with the Bourdains in Portchester for a traditional Brazilian dinner of *feijoada* and cheese rolls. Feijoada is the national dish of Brazil and takes a lot of ingredients, but it is worth the time it takes to shop and cook.

The cheese rolls are super-easy to make once you purchase the tapioca flour, and they are a real treat for gluten-intolerant folks.

BRAZILIAN CHEESE ROLLS

INGREDIENTS

1/2 cup olive oil
2 cups tapioca flour
2 tsp. minced garlic
2/3 cup Parmesan cheese
2 beaten eggs
1/3 cup water
1/3 cup milk
1 tsp. salt

DIRECTIONS

Preheat oven to 375°. Pour olive oil, water, milk, and salt into a large saucepan over high heat. When the mixture comes to a boil, remove from heat immediately and stir in tapioca flour and garlic until smooth. Set aside to rest for 10–15 minutes. Drop by the tablespoon on to a greased cookie sheet, leaving 2 inches between them. Bake in preheated oven until the tops are lightly browned or for about 15–20 minutes. Serve warm with butter.

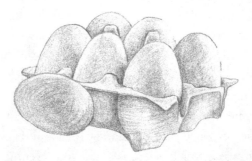

Adam was a freshman at Manhattanville College, which was only twenty minutes away, so he could come home whenever he wanted but was living at school. Zach was very busy in high school, as was Toby in middle school. Elizabeth was busy with after-school activities and play dates, and I was teaching cooking classes and had begun writing a weekly column for the *Larchmont Gazette* called "Dine and Wine." It was a hectic time, but I enjoyed writing about my life and offering recipes. I was often stopped in town by people who had read the column.

One of the most appreciated recipes published in the *Gazette* was for potato latkes. They are simple enough to make, but like most recipes with few ingredients, it is the preparation that makes all the difference between outstanding and ordinary. I learned to make these potato pancakes from my mother, who really was an amazing cook. I like to grind the potatoes, which I do with the KitchenAid attachment, but my mother used her meat grinder. I have very strong memories of standing over the meat grinder, shoving potato and onion slices into it while my brother turned the handle over and over.

POTATO LATKES

INGREDIENTS

4 large potatoes, peeled
1 large onion, peeled
1 egg, beaten
2 Tbs. flour
1 tsp. baking powder
1 tsp. salt, or more to taste
1/2 tsp. black pepper
Vegetable oil for frying
Apple sauce and/or sour cream

DIRECTIONS

Pour enough vegetable oil into a frying pan so that it is 1 inch deep. Heat to 375° on a frying thermometer. If using a hand grater, grate the potatoes and onion on the largest circular openings of the hand grater. If using a food processor, grate the potatoes and onion with the grating attachment, and then take all but 1 cup of the mixture and chop coarsely using the metal blade.

Now add the grated mixture to the chopped mixture. If using a grinder, simply grind the potatoes and onion together. Pour this mixture into a colander and allow to drain for a few minutes. Pour back into the bowl and add the remaining ingredients. Using a large spoon, drop the batter carefully into the hot oil, allowing room between the latkes so as not to overcrowd the pan. Be sure to maintain a temperature of 375°. Carefully turn the latkes over after the bottoms have browned and brown on the other side. Serve immediately with applesauce. They may be reheated in a moderate oven, or frozen.

SERVES 4–6

The measure of how great the latkes were in the house where I grew up was how many you could eat. In other words, was it a two latke-latke, or a three or four latke-latke? There are houses divided over whether latkes should be eaten with applesauce or sour cream. I grew up eating them with apple sauce and cannot fathom why anyone would eat an oily dish like potato pancakes with more fat. For me, the applesauce cuts the grease with some acid.

Using nearly the same recipe, my mother and grandmothers, like almost all Eastern European Jews, made potato kugel. Kugel means *pudding* in German, and although this is not a sweet dish, it is baked in a casserole, giving it a pudding appearance. My mother had many secrets (which she happily shared with me) for her crispy on the outside, soft on the inside, salty, oniony, delicious potato kugel. One of her secrets was putting the empty pan with chicken fat (schmaltz) into the hot oven for a few minutes, and then pouring the batter into it, making the bottom and sides crisp.

One year, I asked my mother to bring her potato kugel to our Passover Seder. We were all enjoying it immensely when I asked her what her secret was to making her Passover kugel so crisp. It was hard for me to imagine that she could achieve that crispness using the prescribed matzo meal in place of the usual flour, as it was not permissible to use flour for Passover. She happily recited her recipe, using the usual flour in her kugel. I was shocked that she ignored the rules and had used forbidden flour in it, but she did not see the point in a soggy crust so she used her tried-and-true recipe, Passover be damned! Pretty funny now—not so much then!

POTATO KUGEL

INGREDIENTS

4 large Idaho potatoes
1 large onion
2 eggs
1/3 cup chicken fat or oil
2 1/2 Tbs. matzo meal
2 tsp. baking powder
1 1/2 tsp. salt
1 tsp. black pepper
Applesauce

DIRECTIONS

Preheat oven to 375°. Grind or grate the potatoes and onion together in a grinder, food processor or grater. If using a food processor, move the mixture to a bowl and replace the grating blade with the metal chopping blade. Process the mixture until all large pieces have been chopped, but do not puree. Allow to drain in a colander for 10 minutes.

Place an 8 x 8-inch baking dish that has 1 tablespoon of the fat placed in it into the oven to warm. Beat the eggs in a large bowl. Remove 1 Tbs. of the fat or oil from the remaining fat, and set aside. Add the fat (minus the 1 Tbs.) to the eggs and mix well. Add the drained potatoes and onions to the egg mixture and then add the matzo meal, baking powder, salt, and pepper. Carefully remove the pan from the oven and turn it around, so that the fat is evenly spread around the pan. Pour the potato mixture into the pan, smoothing the top, and bake for 50 minutes. Take the pan from the oven and spread the remaining Tbs. of fat over the surface, spreading it evenly. Bake for 10 minutes or until golden brown. Serve with applesauce, if desired.

SERVES 4–6

Even though my mom was a wonderful cook, she truly did not care about food. She cooked gourmet dinners every night for my father because he loved fancy food, but she was happy with a grilled cheese sandwich. She just didn't care enough to follow what I felt were obvious rules about food. For instance, we were all going to our synagogue for Yom Kippur services and all the congregants were bringing food to break the fast. Mom brought six homemade corn muffins that were dry and stale from having been baked a few days beforehand. I thought that it was a bizarre choice, given the size of the crowd and the need for delicious comfort food after fasting. She did not understand why I would be annoyed; after all, she had made them herself. I decided not to push it. One of the other more appropriate dishes she often brought to the synagogue was a spinach frittata that is incredibly delicious.

SPINACH FRITTATA

INGREDIENTS

2 cups frozen, chopped spinach, defrosted and drained

1 onion, chopped

2 eggs, beaten

1/4 cup matzo meal

4 oz. cottage cheese

6 Tbs. Parmesan cheese

1 cup sour cream or plain yogurt

DIRECTIONS

Preheat oven to 375°. Grease a jelly-roll pan (or low-sided cookie sheet). Combine all ingredients and spread evenly onto pan. Bake until lightly browned, about 45 minutes. Cool slightly and cut into squares. Serve hot with a dollop of sour cream or yogurt. May be prepared ahead and refrigerated or frozen until ready to bake.

SERVES 8–10 AS AN APPETIZER

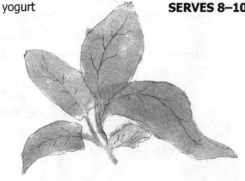

I am writing this on the day after Yom Kippur, many years after the events I have just described. I wish that I could have known how much I would miss my mom and her cardboard spinach frittata. This was my first High Holiday without her and her absence was palpable.

Back when we moved to Westchester, we quickly connected to Chavurah Tikvah and went to our first service in a home nearby. I was completely smitten with the warmth, the songs, the personal style of the service. But I was mostly smitten by the tall, gangly man sitting next to me. He sang with his whole being; a spirituality unlike anyone I had ever met—never mind that he was slightly off-key. Something about him told me that this was a very special man with whom I needed to be connected. It turned out that he was one of the most prominent rabbis of North America and a revered professor at Hebrew Union College. Larry Hoffman is a preeminent scholar and spiritual leader to this day. When we got home from that service, I told Peter that we needed to join the Chavurah, and we joined and stayed with the group for almost twenty-five years.

It turned out that the group only accepted twenty-five families because they held services in their homes and they wanted everyone to have enough room to host the entire group. We needed to be interviewed in order to join, which was a little unnerving. However, during the interview they asked if we liked to cook, as they often held pot-luck suppers. I replied that I LOVE to cook and the two copresidents looked at each other and winked! That was that, we were in!

As I mentioned, services were held in our homes, and the first service we went to as members was celebrating the holiday of *Sukkot*. This is the holiday where we are commanded to build huts (*sukkahs*) and live in them for eight days. This concept works out much better in Israel than in New York, as the holiday comes as autumn sets in. We sat in the backyard of one of the most amazing families in the group for this service, and the husband and wife played guitar and we all sang together. At the end of the service, we were asked to host the next holiday, *Simchat Torah*, which marks the end of the holidays by celebrating the Torah.

We agreed to host it (how could we not), only to realize that the holiday comes only one week after Sukkot. We had only one week to write the service and prepare for seventy-five guests for dessert after the ceremony. It was daunting, but we did not disappoint. At one point in the service, we took the Torah and headed outside to our backyard, with all of us dancing with the Torah around the yard in the dark. It was magical and was remembered for many years to come.

Sukkot is the first time in the fall that I feel like cooking something warming and "stick to your ribs" comfort food. All summer, salad and grilled meat are all that I want to cook and to eat, but when that autumn wind starts blowing, you need food that warms you. One of the most iconic dishes for Sukkot is *cholent*, which is in my opinion a Jewish riff on French *cassoulet*. Cassoulet is a warming dish of beans and potatoes and whatever meat a French peasant has in the kitchen, usually pork sausage, ham hocks, and maybe a duck leg or two.

The Jewish version is basically the same, except that the pork is changed out for beef or chicken. It has been said that the word "cholent" is a corruption of the French word for hot, *chaud*. This dish could be assembled before Shabbat and cooked in the oven for a very long time at a very low temperature to be eaten after sundown. Most people in the time before ovens were a mandatory feature in every kitchen, used the community baker to cook their family's cholent. My mother's father, Papa, grew up in New York City's Lower East Side, and it was his job as a boy to take the family cholent to and from the neighborhood bakery.

CHOLENT

INGREDIENTS

½ cup black-eyed peas, soaked in water to cover overnight

1 Tbs. vegetable oil

1 lb. beef flanken or 1 fryer chicken, cut up—or a combination

3 or 4 beef or veal marrow bones

1 onion, chopped

3 or 4 Idaho potatoes, peeled and chopped

1 Tbs. paprika

1 Tbs. salt

1 onion, diced (to sauté)

Black pepper, 1/2 tsp., or to taste

1 Tbs. vegetable oil

1 carrot, diced

1 parsnip, diced

1 celery stalk, sliced

1 cup pearl barley, washed

1/4 cup ketchup

DIRECTIONS

Preheat oven to 350°. Heat oil in a large, ovenproof casserole and add the beef and bones or the chicken and brown on both sides. Combine the chopped onion, the potatoes, paprika, and salt—and set them aside. Place the diced onions and the black pepper into the pot over medium heat without any oil. When the onions have dried and are beginning to sizzle, then add the oil and fry until light brown and crisp, and add the carrot, parsnip, barley, ketchup—and cook, covered, over medium heat for about 20 minutes or until the water has been absorbed.

To assemble the cholent, first place the meat and bones on the bottom of the pot. Then add layers of the potato, the vegetable-barley mix, and the black-eyed peas, ending with a layer of the vegetable-barley mix. Pour 1/2 cup water mixed with 1 Tbs. salt over the mixture. Add enough water to cover well and bring to a boil. Cover the pot and place in the oven. After 1/2 hour, reduce the oven to 275° and bake for 8 hours, adding more water when it appears dry. Remove meat and bones—dice meat and return to pot.

SERVES 6–8

We left 1 Lancia Lane, in June, practically on the day that Toby graduated high school. The mom of one of his good friends offered to host a graduation party for the two of them. When she asked if I would cook something to bring to the party, I responded that I didn't even have a pot to piss in (which was true). Unfortunately, Toby's graduation came at a very chaotic and difficult time!

CHAPTER 11

188 MOUNT PLEASANT AVENUE
MAMARONECK, NEW YORK
JUNE 2006–JULY 2007

We bought a very small Victorian house in the town of Mamaroneck. It was up the street from the harbor and across the green from the community theater. The kitchen was large in comparison to the size of the house, and that made me very happy. The kitchen window looked out onto a small, but picturesque, backyard.

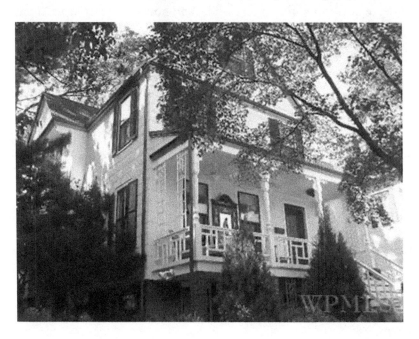

We expected that Toby would be living in the dorm at college, and that Zach would be as well. We bought the house on Mount Pleasant Avenue with the intention of moving upstate within the year and using the house when we needed to be in Westchester. However, there was so much repair work that needed to be done on this 1890s Victorian home that we were forced to spend the summer in the country.

Neither Toby nor Zach were interested in being in the country over the summer, so they spent it in the Mamaroneck house under construction, on couches at friends' houses, or who knows where. After Adam graduated from college, he decided on a career as a chef and earned a degree at the International Culinary Education program and landed a job in Manhattan at Maloney and Porcelli.

Zach spent the fall of that year on a program called Semester at Sea, which took him around the world studying business everywhere from Korea to India, to Turkey, to Spain and Italy. It was not an easy journey, and he returned transformed in a way that only difficult travel can change a person. He told stories of his trips and brought back lovely gifts for us and an enthusiasm for food which he had not ever had before. His favorite dish was Fettuccini Carbonara, which we ate quite often for a short while, and honestly, never again since, because it is so rich (but so delicious).

FETTUCCINI CARBONARA

INGREDIENTS

4 Tbs. unsalted butter, softened
2 whole eggs
2 egg yolks
1 cup freshly grated Parmesan cheese
1 lb. fresh or dried fettuccini
8 slices thick-cut bacon, cut into 1/4-inch pieces
1 tsp. dried hot-pepper flakes
1/2 cup heavy cream
Sea salt and black pepper to taste

DIRECTIONS

Bring a large pot of water to a boil and then add 1 tsp. of salt. When boiling, add the fettuccini and stir often. While the water is boiling, beat the butter in a small bowl with a wooden spoon until fluffy, add the eggs, and whisk until blended—then add half of the parmesan. Fry the bacon in a large skillet until crisp and drain off half the fat. Add the hot pepper and cream and cook over medium heat to bring to a simmer, then turn to low heat and keep warm. When the pasta is just al dente, remove from the water and place it in the skillet with the bacon and cream, mixing to coat thoroughly. Add the egg and cheese mixture and mix well. Add salt, pepper, and the remaining cheese. Taste for seasoning and serve immediately.

SERVES 4

The kitchen window over the sink looked out onto our neighbor's home. They were a lovely young family from Pakistan. The neighbors on the other side of the house were two teachers; the husband was Elizabeth's music teacher, named Steph. He is a great cook and the child of immigrants from China. I invited him to coteach a class on wonton soup with me at the high-school adult-education course.

It was the only class I have ever taught in over twenty years that I considered a disaster. One of the students was a woman whose son had signed her up for the class. She was clearly suffering from dementia, as she spoke loudly to herself for the entire class. It completely threw me, but Steph didn't even seem to notice her as he patiently taught us how to make the wontons. I suppose that teaching music to elementary-age children requires one to be an extremely patient person.

CHINN FAMILY WONTON SOUP

INGREDIENTS

3–4 dried black mushrooms, soaked in hot water

2 scallions, cut into 1-inch pieces

1/4 cup canned water chestnuts, drained

1 lb. boneless pork, cut into 1-inch pieces

1 lb. shrimp, peeled and deveined (if frozen, defrosted)

1 1/2 tsp. kosher salt

1 Tbs. tamari soy sauce

1 1/2 tsp. sherry or mirin (sweetened cooking wine)

1 tsp. toasted sesame oil

1 Tbs. fresh ginger, peeled and minced

1 egg

2 1-lb. wonton wrappers (about 90)

1/3 cup chicken broth per person

1/2 lb. Asian greens

DIRECTIONS

Remove stems from the softened mushrooms and cut into small pieces. Put all ingredients (except wrappers and chicken broth) into a food processor fitted with the metal blade, and pulse until the mixture is coarsely ground. Place one teaspoon of filling into a wrapper and fold according to instructions. For soup, boil for 5 minutes in water and then place into heated chicken broth, adding the roast pork and Asian greens, cook five more minutes.

SERVES 8

Steph and I often had friendly food competitions, and I can remember one over chicken Scarpariello, which was a lot of fun and very delicious.

CHICKEN SCARPARIELLO

INGREDIENTS

1/4 cup olive oil

2 Tbs. unsalted butter

2 Italian-style sausages (chicken or pork), cut into 1/2 inch-thick slices

6 chicken thighs, with bone and skin, chopped in half with a cleaver

1 head garlic, peeled and coarsely chopped

8 jarred hot cherry peppers, halved

8 jarred sweet red peppers, halved

1/2 cup dry white wine

2 Tbs. balsamic vinegar

1/2 cup chicken stock

1 Tbs. fresh or 1 1/2 tsp. dried oregano

Sea salt and freshly ground black pepper, to taste

Lemon juice, to taste

DIRECTIONS

Heat a large skillet over moderately high heat and add the oil and butter. When the butter has melted, add the sausages and chicken and brown lightly on all sides. Lower the heat and continue to cook, turning the chicken every few minutes, then add the garlic and the peppers, cooking until the chicken is no longer pink when poked with a sharp knife. Remove the contents and add the wine, vinegar, chicken stock, and oregano—stirring them in thoroughly. Add salt and pepper and taste for seasoning—and cook a few more minutes until the sauce has reduced somewhat. Turn off the heat and add the lemon juice. Pour the sauce over the chicken and serve.

SERVES 8

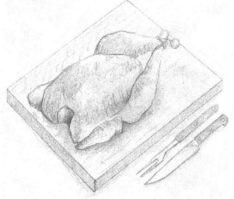

We had friends a block away, the community theater was across the street, the harbor was two blocks away, and the center of town was literally down the hill. All in all, it was a great place to live. Toby started college nearby, but he preferred to live at home. However, Elizabeth's time at Mamaroneck Avenue School began to come to an end, so we started our research into schools in the Hillsdale area. We were certain that raising her in the country would be better than in Westchester. We believed that she would be happier in a more relaxed atmosphere that concentrated on nature and the arts—and not the intense academic pressure that the boys had experienced at Mamaroneck High School.

After several disappointing experiences, we discovered a wonderful school only five minutes from our house. The instant we walked into Hawthorne Valley School, we all knew that it was the right fit. We didn't know anything about Waldorf education at the time, but the art on the walls, the music in the air, and even the architecture exuded a strong dedication to the arts. This was just what she and we needed for her education and a change in lifestyle for the three of us.

It was January of 2007 when we visited Hawthorne Valley School and enrolled Elizabeth for the following fall. We left the house on Mount Pleasant Avenue in late June with great expectations for the future and a good touch of sadness for the present.

Peter, Toby, me, Mom, Dad, and Elizabeth

CHAPTER 12

214 DAWSON ROAD
HILLSDALE, NEW YORK
JULY 2007–PRESENT

We moved into the house on Dawson Road in the summer and immediately began to plan the renovations. The house had been built in the 1860s as a one-room schoolhouse and was sorely in need of refreshing. There was orange Formica on the counters in the kitchen and no window at all in the kitchen. The only window nearby was in the laundry space off the kitchen. There was no bathroom upstairs and the living space was tiny in the winter when the screened-in porch was unusable.

Me and Elizabeth, December 2007

We had three contractors tell us to tear the house down, but the fourth said we needed to preserve the history of the place. Naturally we hired him. However, on the first day of the renovations he discovered cracks in the foundation, mold in the basement, and rotten floorboards. We ended up nearly tearing the whole house down, anyway. The picture above shows the space where the kitchen, laundry, and living room had been. The small window at the back was the only source of natural light in the kitchen.

We could not live through a renovation so dramatic, so we once again needed to move. We rented a small cabin in Copake Falls and drove the half hour back and forth each day to check on the work and to take Elizabeth back and forth from school. The cabin was very sweet but so tiny that Elizabeth's bed took up her entire room. The only bathroom was at the back of the kitchen, which was a long and difficult journey in the middle of the night—from our bedroom, down the hall, down the tiny stairway, through the living room, and through the kitchen.

It was only supposed to take nine months for our renovations, so we thought that would be fine. When nine months turned into eighteen months, the charm of the place grew old. One week before Elizabeth's Bat Mitzvah, which was to be held at home, we moved back into our beautiful newly renovated house on Dawson

Bat Mitzvah-time

Road. The house ended up even better than we could have imagined, and it is definitely the home that embodies our spirit in every detail. We had not even finished moving into the house as we hosted the party for over a hundred guests. The Bat Mitzvah was a celebration in every sense of the word, and a marvelous time was had by all.

After the event, our

contractor and his craftsmen returned to finish the work. I decided that it would be very disruptive to my family to teach cooking in our house, so we designed a teaching kitchen that was adjacent to the garage. It ended up being not only the perfect place to teach but also to cook for family events, such as Passover, and to eventually do catering. I held classes every month on a schedule, as well as requested by individuals. I also taught at private homes for birthday parties, at a local kitchen store, and at public events, such as farmer's markets, and I had a regular gig at Olana, the estate of the renowned Hudson River School artist, Frederic Church.

It was not easy teaching at Olana, as they had no kitchen at all, so I had to bring absolutely everything with me, down to the spoons. It is a distance from the house and they paid very little, but the students were lovely, and it was a beautiful place to teach. One year they included me in their anniversary celebration for several decades of significance, including the sixties era. For the event, I prepared a gelatin mold with wine and fruit that was a huge success. My kids later told me that it was a "jello shot"!

GELATIN SHOTS

INGREDIENTS

3 Tbs. gelatin powder, dissolved in 1/4 cup cold water then added to 3/4 cup hot water
1/2 cup fine white sugar
1 3/4 cup fruit juice (cranberry, grape, orange, etc.)
1 cup white wine
1 cup fruit (sliced strawberries, halved grapes, pitted cherries, melon balls, etc.)

DIRECTIONS

Add the sugar to the gelatin mixture and stir until it is dissolved. Add the juice and the wine and mix thoroughly. Pour into mini muffin tins and refrigerate for half an hour. Stir in the fruit and chill until set. Place the tins in a bowl of hot water for 30 seconds and then place a plate over the top of the tin and invert.

SERVES 4

The teaching kitchen ended up as a great space that I have enjoyed using these past twelve years. In it I have taught over one hundred classes for hundreds of students and catered five weddings, countless events, and our own family occasions. Having this space gives me a place to cook a wonderful meal while leaving the kitchen in the house perfectly clean.

The teaching kitchen

Adam moved to Hudson and is now working as a butcher in Kingston and living with his wonderful girlfriend, Lacey. Zach married his Polish girlfriend, Roza, went to medical school and became an Emergency Specialist. Toby earned a Master's degree in Transpersonal Counseling Psychology in Boulder, Colorado and has stayed there with his new bride, Brittany. Elizabeth went to university in Montreal, studying Theatre Creation, and then received a master's degree in Performance Studies from the University of London, Goldsmith College, where she still resides.

My parents struggled with their relationship in their final years, and we arranged for my mother to stay in an assisted living facility near us, while my father remained in Manhattan. He declined very quickly and died at the age of eighty-eight. My mother remained in her assisted living home with a lot of help for another four years. We began to travel after my father died and were in China when we got word that my mother was near the end. It took four planes and two days to get there, but we made it back before she passed.

As I write this today, it would have been my mother's ninetieth birthday. Her older sister, Roda, passed away this week at ninety-four. Roda was the last of her generation, and with her passing, my generation become the elders.

Zach and Roza have a son, Artemus Wallace, who is now almost two years old. (Wallace was my dad's name.) Artemus has a brand-new brother, named Kazimir Edward. Kazimir was the name of many Polish kings and Edward is in memory of Peter's father. We wish them abundant health and sleep.

We have just lived through the Covid pandemic, which brought immeasurable suffering to so many. But for me, it gave me precious time with my children and my incredible husband. Without him, my life would have been so empty. This time at home has given me the space to do the many things that have waited on the shelf. This book is the result of the time that I was gifted.

I was blessed with the time and space to write down the events of my life that were worth sharing. It took me almost ten years and a pandemic, but this chapter is now done. Time to turn my attention from the past to the future. Now it is *my* turn to be the Nana or Bubbe. (I can't decide which I will be called.)

(Not) The End

Artemus Wallace and Zach

ACKNOWLEDGMENTS

This book started out as a pile of handwritten recipes by my grand-mothers, Anna and Sarah, and my mother, Lora. This pile of notes needed to be organized and categorized. I immediately felt called upon to honor the recipes by connecting them to the stories of the people who created them. When I cook their recipes for family and friends, their legacy continues. Thank you to all my dear extended family and wonderful friends who make my life so sweet and spicy!

As a first-time writer, I am very grateful to my editor, Dory Mayo, and my book designer, Colin Rolfe, whose knowledge and experience have brought this ten-year journey to its conclusion. Thank you for all your encouragement and guidance.

My deep thanks go to my sweet and talented son, Tobias, for the beautiful illustrations he drew for this book. I cannot remember a more generous gift. Toby and his three siblings, Adam, Zachary, and Elizabeth inspired me every day to attempt to put a delicious dinner on the table. Spending time together in the kitchen with my children continues to be the greatest joy in my life.

Thank you to my loving husband, Peter, for forty-nine years of tasting, listening, and endless patience and caring!

INDEX OF RECIPES

ABOUT THE AUTHOR

Julie Gale opened the At the Kitchen Table Cooking School in 2001 in Westchester County, New York. At the same time, she wrote the food column, "Dine and Wine," for the *Larchmont Gazette* and was the recipe developer for the children's book, *I Want to Cook*.

Gale has taught cooking as a guest at Williams College; the Olana (NY) State Historic Site; A Different Drummer; and the Chef's Shop in Great Barrington, Massachusetts. She previously held the position of cooking instructor at the Hawthorne Valley Waldorf School, and was Retreat Chef at the Won Dharma Center in Claverack, New York, for several years.

After receiving a master's degree in Community Social Work from Yeshiva University, Gale also maintained a private practice that advised parents through the Special Education process in Westchester County. She ultimately moved to Columbia County in the northern Hudson Valley region and now lives in rural Hillsdale, New York, with her husband, Peter. Together, they have four grown children who currently reside in Hudson, New York; Nashville, Tennessee; Boulder, Colorado; and London, England.

The author can be reached at atthekitchentable@fairpoint.net.

Printed in the USA
CPSIA information can be obtained
at www.ICGtesting.com
JSHW02074322 1023
50375JS00001B/38